The Adventures of
BENNY BOB

Ben R. Games, PhD

© Copyright 2010,
Ben R. Games, PhD

Revised Edition

All Rights Reserved.

No part of this book may be reproduced in any form or by any means, stored in a retrieval system, or be transmitted by any means, electronic or mechanical; this includes photocopying, recording, or otherwise, without written permission from the author. For information, contact Fideli Publishing at www.FideliPublishing.com

ISBN-13: 978-1-60414-000-2
ISBN-10: 1-60414-000-3

Contents

AUTHOR'S STATEMENT 5
FACTS 9
PROLOGUE 12
BUILDING BLOCKS 15
THE PACK-TRAIN 21
THE WALKING STICK..................... 32
DYNAMITE 74
NAVAHO CLIFF HIEROGLYPHICS 93
MOTHER'S RING 100
THE PIGS STRATAGEM 109
A GRANDFATHER'S PRAYER.................114
THE GUARDIAN ANGEL 117
ENDURANCE...119
FORWARD, SHANGRI-LA VIETNAM..... 120
SHANGRI-LA VIETNAM 123
FUUJIN... 125
RICHES 127
EAST & WEST BERLIN 131
BEYOND THE MILKY WAY.................... 145
AUTHORS PERSONAL INFORMATION..... 155

Games Family

Betty Jo

Young Ben

Benny Bob

Aircraft Commander B-29

The war department today announced the promotion of Ben Robert Games of Elkhart to first lieutenant. Lt. Games is first pilot of a B-29 Superfortress, and has been stationed at Roswell, N. Mex. His wife, Helen, and son, Ben, Jr., returned to Elkhart several weeks ago after being with him, and are residing at 221 State. Lt. Games' parents, Mr. and Mrs. Robert Games, live at 503 Sunset.

The Adventures of Benny Bob

AUTHOR'S STATEMENT

Authors:
Ben R. Games, PhD
Helen M. Games, MBA
Elizabeth M. Baker, BA
Betty Jo Games
Jeff G. Amsden
Mathew A. Knight

These are autobiographical adventure stories about growing up in the wild, wild west where Young Benny Bob's sense of humor taught him to run fast. It's actually a series of events showing how Benny Bob lived and later became a citizen soldier. This may be a clue to how a boy growing up can developed into a great warrior in a time of world confusion.

These stories are based upon journal entries and pictures taken of Benny Bob's adventures by his mother and later his wife. Readers of these stories may think that Benny Bob was a mean little kid, but this was not true. It was only that he was bored and hated to carry buckets of water. As a young man he was always wondering if there was another way of doing things, and he is still seeking a better way.

Today we live in a Geo-feudal age. An age where there are chairmen instead of kings, politicos instead of knights, and stockholders instead of serfs. History shows us that this age started sometime after WW II, when our congress was mostly made up of military veterans who believed everyone who served our country should have the opportunity to earn a college education.

At the time when Benny Bob was growing up, all young men were drafted, and every man or woman after serving their country was given the GI Bill to pay for a college education at the school of his choice.

Another title for this work might be, "The Clan's Voice" because the poems and stories were all written by the members of the Games Clan in their own words. Some of it was written before they were transferred to the Corps of Angels.

For God and Country,
Ben R. Games, PhD

Helen and Ben Games

Ben R. Games, PhD, Major, CW-4, TCNA-6 and Helen M. Games, MBA, in the Fiji Islands, 1966. They were on a speaking tour about the Vietnam War.

FACTS

The author, Ben R. Games, PhD, has written many books, some are semi-biographical and some are not. He starts each of his stories with a chapter about one of his experiences while growing up.

As a young man, his friends would call him Benny Bob. When he became an Army aviator in Vietnam, it was Gentle Ben. The author thought that the troopers called him Gentle Ben because he is a gentle man. Then, one day he heard Radio Vietnam TV air a program that had a bear named Gentle Ben in it. Only then did he learn why the Cavalry Troopers gave him the nickname Gentle Ben — they thought that he turned into a bear when the enemy was shooting at his helicopter. They were right of course. **That's a FACT.**

During the author's childhood his parents lived in the western United States at the time when the Hoover (Boulder) Dam near Boulder City, Nevada, was being built. Historians call this time "The Great Depression." People often died from hunger during this period, so finding food for the family was the main job of the men and boys. The author's father worked at many jobs, including bootlegger, prospector, miner, blacksmith, and a member of the US Geological Survey Gang running a pack-train of burros. **That's a FACT.**

Benny Bob's mother, Betty Jo, would make a sandwich out of her homemade bread, spread it with pig lard, and then sprinkle the lard with sugar. She told him that if he put his first two fingers on the bread and then fold the bread over them, it was a "Finger Sandwich." He would get one finger sandwich and all the water he could drink at noon. Sometimes his mother would cry a little as she fed him. **That's a FACT.**

A loaf of bread had to last the family for a week, so Benny Bob could only have one slice at noon. When it was time for supper, he got two slices of bread broken up in a bowel and sprinkled with sugar, then canned milk mixed with water was poured over it. His working father, Bob, got beans, a slice of bread, and a piece of Mountain Sheep jerky. **That's a FACT.**

For breakfast, Young Ben got to eat any beans that were left from the evening meal, and a glass of Ovaltine. To this day, the author likes Ovaltine, beans, homemade bread and milk. **That's a FACT.**

During World War II, the Australians furnished cans of mutton to everyone fighting the Japanese in the Pacific. The author got mutton gravy on toast for breakfast, mutton gravy over beans with rice for lunch, and all the mutton he could eat at supper. He definitely looked forward to Sunday dinner because Spam was on the menu! **That's a FACT.**

PROLOGUE

The Adventures of Benny Bob is a collection of true stories. The people are real and the events really happened. It is also true that the story is semi-biographical, since the author was known as Bobby, Benny Bob, and now Ben.

There are times, though, when the author tells a story where the enemy's name, weight or height is changed and sometimes even his nationality is not mentioned. The author is not trying to change history, he wants to tell how he and his family lived in it. He is quick to acknowledge that most young men who grew up to become citizen soldiers did not serve our country as he did. The author believes that if you put yourself in Benny Bob's shoes you would have done as he did.

The author has also written fiction. The science fiction stories *Beyond* and *Galaxy Slaves* are pure off the wall fiction, even if they are based on facts obtained while working with the Aero Medical Labs, Wright Patterson AFB, Dayton, Ohio. All Ben did was take this knowledge; add conjecture to form a story of why, how, and maybe. Let's hope he is wrong, not making true prophetic utterances.

One time Ben learned that an island country's government was meeting with a communist nation's representatives who were attempting to stop the United States' space program. On the day he learned that the leaders of both island countries were having a secret conference, he flew to the communist island straight away.

The Chief of the island's Secret Service met Ben at the airport and escorted him to the village where the meeting was taking place. It was midnight when he arrived at the meeting site, and there was another hour of discussion after that before he was allowed to speak.

At two in the morning on a dark night, he sat on a log between the chief minister and the minister of labor. A large wood fire was the only light as he argued for support of the United States. When dawn broke, NASA had its down range radar site.

Ben has written about this adventure, but few will believe it except for the people who were there. It is a semi-biographical adventure so the reader can enjoy the story without worrying about history or State Department protocol.

BUILDING BLOCKS

Ben R. Games, PhD

History is a window looking into the future.

Pilots of the Army Class of 43K have served in world wars that almost destroyed civilization. Now we have a chance to help our children's children by telling our stories so that they may peek into their future. We may think our stories are dull, uninteresting, or of no value, but that's not true.

Let me assure you that someone sometime will read your journal and find the inspiration to help others. The readers of your journal may ask themselves, "How can anyone be that stupid or brilliant." No matter what the reader thinks of your story, it will give them a chance to see a little of how you lived history. My stories will not change history. They are only about how I lived in it. Today is yesterday's history, and the building blocks for a window that can show the future.

Helen and I are Hoosiers. We met in Goshen, Indiana, when I was home on leave from the Army in September 1942. After 44 years 5 months and 28 days service in the Army & USAF, she is still trying to keep me out of trouble. Today she and Montana, a black Labrador guide dog, have joined forces to try to keep me from falling on my face.

One thing that may be different about Helen compared to other 43-K members' wives is that she has shared the dirt, misery, and fear of combat at my side in many unusual places. She has made our home in many countries including Vietnam, Japan, Okinawa, France, Texas, and Grand Turk with stops all around the world. I flew bombers and night fighters in WW II, jet fighters during the Korean War, and helicopters during the Vietnam War.

We were married very young and newly wed when I reported to my first duty station at Goodfellow Field in San Angelo, Texas. Helen and I arrived in San Angelo around 2000 hours, and the first thing we did was find a room. The next morning at 0700 hours I reported to the airbase.

The Base Commander, Colonel Gunn, had the Adjutant escort me into his office. A brand new 2nd Lt. reported with a salute, and at 0705 the Colonel asked me what time I had arrived in San Angelo. He then had the Adjutant dock me a day's pay for being late.

During the next 30 minutes, I learned that the Army came first, that as an officer everything in the Army was my responsibility, also if it was Army it was mine, and since enlisted men were part of the Army, I was responsible for them, too. Then he had me sign a hand receipt for two aircraft and five enlisted men. *(I have never forgotten that lesson. Even today I will fight for the rights of soldiers — attack a veteran and you attack me.)*

That following Sunday I took Helen for a ride in my first Army aircraft. It was a BT-13. Someone reported me to Colonel Gunn, and I got to visit him again. During our conversation, he stopped hollering just long enough to ask what I was doing flying an engine test hop with Helen as my passenger. I informed him that he had told me if it was the Army's it was mine, and I was only showing Helen my new aircraft. He then gave me my second lesson on how to think. From that day on I could no longer take my wife on test hops because "I should not expose her to unusual danger. I must think ahead and take her flying on my days off when it did not interfere with the duties of my enlisted men."

Over the years, Helen has flown with me as a copilot in General Creigie's B-25, as an RO in my F82G fighter in Okinawa during the Korean War, in all types of Army helicopters, and in my Chinook in Vietnam. One time we even flew a C-45 on a cross country flight with her mother and sisters as passengers.

Helen later became the 86th woman in the world to fly a helicopter, and got a medal for doing it. She was invited to the White House for tea by Lady Bird Johnson, and another time we had our picture taken with President and Barbara Bush at a dinner in Washington, DC.

Now you may think that I was not in the same Army or Air Force you were, but it really was only that my orders came from a different branch. When I volunteered to join the OSS during WW II, it was with the understanding that I would not leave the Army. I have never had a break in military service, but I never got to fly in the large formations that many of my 43-K classmates did.

My missions were always single aircraft missions. When I needed a crew, they were volunteers — and they sometimes changed on a daily basis. I also got to fly foreign aircraft, and almost every type of civilian aircraft including gliders and balloons. My combat experience is mostly one-on-one and took place where no one would want to be and sometimes before the people at home knew we were fighting.

My biggest problem with the Veterans Administration was trying to convince them that the poison ivy I got was because of Agent Orange and not from parachuting into a swamp after my engine failed. I was 72 years old at the time, and the VA Doctors keep telling me that I should be retired.

Author Ben R. Games in Army OH-58

Road to the Colorado River

The Pack-Train

By Ben R. Games, PhD

1932

There were no bridles for the burros, just halters or a rope to keep them in line. No saddles either, but Benny Bob's burro, Jack, had a pack-saddle (work harness) that cinched around its belly and rump. There was also a forward strap to prevent the pack from slipping off over its tail. It was hard ridding with only a blanket to sit on, especially when Jack took off running flat out to catch up with his mother.

Benny Bob's father was a trained fighter and used his fists to settle arguments. He also had the ability to use a pistol and rifle. He would have

Benny Bob's Father

Benny Bob wear a shoulder holster with a .45 caliber revolver in it. Instead of wearing it where it should be, it was carried on his back under a very loose shirt. Whenever they were with other bootleggers or where his father might need a weapon fast, Benny Bob would stand next to his father for easy access. In practice when his father grabbed the weapon, he would fall down and roll away. The gun was worn many times, but never used.

It took all day to drive from Las Vegas to the Colorado River watering point and base camp.

Planting trees along the side of road to Boulder City

At the camp, there was a wooden platform built back about 50 feet from the river's edge. On it were ten 55 gallon wooden barrels with the tops cut out. Each day the barrels were filled with river water that was full of mud. The water was left until the following day so the mud could settle to the bottom. Clean water was then drawn out, and poured into five gallon canvas water bags.

The outside of the bags were kept wet until the pack-train started out. This kept the water cool. Four water bags were placed on each pack animal with the other supplies tied on top of the packsaddle.

Each survey team was made up of three to five men and each packtrain had at lest ten burros in it. It was planned so that each man had at least ten gallons of water per day. A delivery

of supplies and water was made every other day.

As the survey teams moved further from the watering point, it took longer to make the trip. Because of the high canyon walls and the lack of places to get water, the back-train grew to twenty burros. To control the burros, his father walked leading them. Benny Bob and his mother rode their burros at the end of the train following the pack animals. Benny Bob's burro carried a rolled up blanket, their two jackets, and a bag of jerky on its packsaddle.

Benny Bob wore a metal cloth-covered canteen and a small bull whip around his waist. The end of the whip was split with three leather knotted tips. He could hit a rattlesnake or scorpion with that tip and kill it every time. He wore a big straw hat, shirt with long sleeves, shorts, and heavy walking shoes.

His mother's burro carried her, two one-gallon canvas water bags, and a small cloth-covered canteen. She wore a light dress and a large cloth-brimmed hat. Because they had no saddles, they couldn't carry their walking sticks.

When his mother had to pee, it had to be done in the middle of the trail where the burros had just walked. A dress was the proper attire for this time and need.

They were one day out of base camp and another day from Las Vegas. If someone got bitten by a rattlesnake, there was no way to get help even if they could make it back to camp, because the survey crew had to have water to survive.

Benny Bob's burro was the one-year-old son of the burro his mother rode. It had never

been weaned, and it never let its mother get out of sight. As they rode through the canyons and over the mountain trails the burro would stop to nibble a bit of cactus, weed, or dried grass. Benny Bob tried to make it catch up to the pack-train and its mother by kicking, hitting, or even using the whip, but he couldn't make it move. However just as soon as its mother's tail started to disappear around a bend or rock, Jack went from full stop to full run until his muzzle could touch her. That burro had only two speeds: stop or full speed ahead.

Sometimes the trail was so narrow and the cliffs so high that it didn't seem like he could make the turns at full speed, but Jack never missed a step. When he couldn't find anything else to nibble on, that damn fool burro would turn and bite his rider. Benny Bob spent his days hanging on, trying to keep from being eaten by a burro, and daydreaming.

Imagination is a wonderful thing. At night the sky above Arizona and Nevada was bright with stars, and you could believe that there were spaceships up there, that people lived on Mars and some day men would walk on the moon. In the daytime, Benny Bob would daydream about how he had saved the pack-train by fighting off space invaders or outlaws.

When near the surveyors' camp, they would find a large boulder to rest on where they could wait for the pack-train to return. Why a large rock instead of shade from the desert sun? Snakes like shade and avoid the sun. Sometimes mountain sheep would come near the boulder as they went on up into the mountains.

The mother burro was always hobbled, and when wild horses came up, she was even tied. Her colt, Jack, was never tied because he wouldn't leave his mother. The water canteen and his pack-saddle with the supplies were taken off while waiting for the pack-train to return. One to three hours would pass before the trip home began.

As the surveying camps got further from the river, it took longer to make the round trip. Soon Benny Bob and his mother had to stay by the river preparing for the next trip while his father ran the pack-trains into the mountains alone.

A pack-train had to leave everyday to keep two survey gangs working. His father would start at daylight and wouldn't get back until after dark. Benny Bob and his mother would stay in camp, fill the barrels with water, and get the canteens ready for the next day.

On this trip his father was tired and had hung his canteen with his pistol on a burro's packsaddle. Before, he had always made everyone carry their own canteen and weapons, but this trip was different. The packtrain was following the lead burro, and he was walking along following them as they headed towards base camp. It was the hottest part of the day, around 1500 hours,

when he needed water. He reached for the canteen, and the burro trotted ahead just out of his reach. This went on for over an hour with that stupid burro staying just three feet out of reach.

They were soon coming to a place on the trail where one burro couldn't pass another. His father knew when they got to that point the burro couldn't run ahead and he could catch up. He walked along waiting and planning what he would do to that burro when he got his pistol.

They finely arrived at the narrow part of the trail, and his father ran forward trying to catch hold of the packsaddle. The burro just nipped the burro ahead of him, making all the other burros run down the trail. His father couldn't get within three feet of the water and pistol. He realized then that there was no way he was going to get the canteen.

So, he got smart and found a big rock where he could get some shade and rest. Any rattlesnake around would just have to take its chances. He had to have protection from the hot sun, so he stopped and the whole pack-train stopped with him. He waited for dark because he knew there were not going to be any more stops on the way back to camp.

As soon as the sun set, he started down the trail with the burro staying just out of reach. He never got closer to it than three feet until they arrived at the river. By then it was 2300 hours, and he had been on the trail for over ten hours without water.

Benny Bob and his mother met his father as he arrived in camp. He fell head first into one of the barrels of drinking water causing the barrel to tip over. He splashed water all over himself. He still hadn't spoken to anyone, but as soon as he could stand up, he reached for Benny Bob's rifle and without a word shot that stupid burro dead. Then he walked over to the body, took the canteen it was carrying and started to drink.

***

These experiences helped the author make decisions that he followed for all of his military career: Never fight unless it was to win; never hit someone with your fist if a club is handy; never leave a live enemy behind you; protect the people who work for you; and most importantly, never trust a jackass to help when you're in trouble and *always* carry your own canteen.

In other words, don't wait until you see the whites of their eyes to shoot, have the Air Force drop a bomb instead.

THE WALKING STICK

Memory of events after they happen are kept locked in your brain, and placed in an order determined by a traumatic event, love, or other strong emotion. This must be true or psychologists would be out of a job. Think about it. Remember when you were first taught to wipe your behind after going to the bathroom. If you do, it had to fit into one of these events.

Benny Bob's bus to Las Vegas

Adventures of Benny Bob

It was the time of The Great Depression. Kids ate bread with sugar and lard instead of butter. There was no money and jobs were hard to find. Benny Bob and his mother were staying with grandmother in Los Angeles while his father was making Desert Dew in Nevada.

One bright and sunny morning, a normal day in June 1930, she put Benny Bob on a bus going to Las Vegas and told her son that his father would meet him there. She also told him that she was going to hitchhike a ride at a truck stop and would meet them the next day. Young Ben was only six years old, and it was his first trip by himself. He wondered why it took all night for a truck to make the trip when a bus only took half of a day.

Later he learned that in 1930, the only time a truck driver would pick up a hitchhiker was late in the day because they drove across the desert at night when it was cool. Even at night, they had to stop at various times for an hour or so just to let the truck's engine cool down, especially if they had a heavy load. In those days, they didn't have a sleep-in cab, but the truck drivers all carried a tarp and blanket so they could rest while the truck cooled off.

Women could not hitch hike on the open road but there was no law saying they couldn't ask for a ride. Normally the driver would share a sandwich and beer with the rider. Men usually traveled by catching a ride on a freight train. This wasn't approved of by the railroads, but there were so many people out of work that some of the trains stopping in Las Vegas had from 20 to 100 men riding the rails looking for work building the Hoover Dam. The grounds in front of the depot looked like a hobo town at night after the trains had passed.

Ben's father picked him up at the bus station, and they walked up Frontier Street to the Railroad Depot. On the way, his father stopped at the Golden Nugget Casino and purchased a nickel beer while Benny Bob waited outside on the street. When his father came out of the casino, he carried a boiled egg, cheese and crackers in his pants pocket. This was free bar food, and his father gave it to him for supper.

By the time they got to the Railroad Depot, it was time to sleep. They stopped at a building with a sign that advertised "Beds for Rent—Ten Cents." His father gave the man two dimes, and they were taken into a large room to sleep. The beds were about two feet apart and filled the whole room. They were single cots with a mattress covered with vinyl cloth but no blankets.

Colorado River

All of the men slept in one room, and the women slept in another. There was only one bathroom, so the men peed in the alley. The next day, Benny Bob's mother showed up. His father and mother had a loud argument out on the street in front of the flophouse. His father asked how many trucks she had to hitch a ride on, and when she told him two, he got very mad.

Young Ben's father had a 1929 Model "A" Ford two door. He had it parked in a vacant lot next to a grocery store. His mother and father fought and shopped at the same time. Benny Bob

Benny Bob's father

followed along wondering what he had done to cause all this.

Young Ben had already learned that you peed in alleys, and now he learned that you did the other in vacant lots. His father showed him how to cover the shit with dirt. He was told that this was only polite, and if he had paper to wipe with, the dirt would keep the paper from blowing into people's yards. This Benny Bob could understand. Who wants shitty paper in their yard?

Young Ben was taught another thing that day. As they shopped, his mother showed him how to check the food cans to see if they were bulging at the ends. If they bulged, the food inside was bad. The grocery store owner told them that he would sell these cans of food to them for three cents a can, but Ben's mother said no.

His father bought three sticks of dynamite, two 50-pound bags of sugar, dried apricots, pea-

Base camp.

nut butter, flour, potatoes, dried beans, Ovaltine, and cases of canned goods. His mother also insisted that his father purchase a roll of toilet paper. The storeowner gave his father a Sears and Roebuck Catalog and his father said that would do just as well for boys.

After loading the car, they searched the trash looking for empty bottles. In the afternoon, they went looking for empty whiskey bottles behind the casinos. They finished loading the unused space in the car with the empty bottles. After filling all of the canteens and checking to be sure the tent and two cots were loaded on top of the front fenders, they were ready to go.

Benny Bob's father told him that it looked like there wasn't enough room for him, so Young

Ben made sure that when the car was loaded there was just enough room for him to slide in on top of everything. The last things his father strapped on the fenders were a shovel and a surveyor's transit.

The car was loaded and they were ready to leave, but it was late in the afternoon. There were no roads, so they would have to camp in the desert the first night. The next day they would head for old Fort Calswell and the Colorado River.

Benny Bob's father drove about 10 miles towards the Colorado River before finding a place to camp. He set up the tent, not to keep out rain, but to keep out the snakes. The tent had a floor that was on the ground as well as a door that was six inches above the floor. The door could be zipped closed with the flap still open. This way no snakes could get in.

Father told them that when they got to the river and base camp everyone would get a Walking Stick. Benny Bob wasn't sure what they were for, but decided they must be a good thing because everyone was going to get one.

Once again, Young Ben was worried; there were only two cots. His father told him he guessed Benny Bob would just have to sleep outside. Young Ben's mother told her son not to worry and had his father move four cases of canned goods into the tent. They placed these under one of the cots to help hold it up. They were laughing as they worked, but Young Ben never found out why.

Benny Bob's Father's partner, Leroy Johnson, slept outside under the stars.

Later that night, he woke up hearing his mother groaning. She must have been hurting awful. Young Ben could hardly see in the dark, but peeking out from under his blanket there was enough light to see that his father was on top holding her down. Benny Bob stayed very quite until she stopped groaning before he went back to sleep. He was wakened twice more that night. By daylight, it seemed that his mother was a lot better, and they were ready for the desert again.

Road to Colorado River and Mountain Dew Co.

They drove following the tracks his father had made when he drove to Las Vegas. The only problem was that the wind had blown most of them away. Some of the washes his father drove in had changed since the last time he'd been there. His father would set up the surveyor's transit and sight it on a landmark that he knew, then check a compass as he drove.

Sometimes he would have to stop and use the shovel to cover holes or clear rocks out of the path. It was slow, hot work. They had started at

Desert Dew Co. Parking Lot

daybreak, and by late in the afternoon his father had found a level space in a canyon that would completely hide the car. His father stopped and told them that they were home.

It didn't look like much to Benny Bob, but everyone loaded up with all they could carry and followed his father out of the wash. They could feel the temperature getting cooler, and suddenly, the sun was hidden behind a canyon wall. They could hear the roar of rushing water. It was awesome. It was great. Before them was the mighty Colorado River: *"Maker of the Grand Canyon; Color me brown; Make me so fast that no one can swim against my current; Hide me with walls of rock so high the sun can't warm me; Call me Colorado. Tame me if you can."*

His father set their tent back from the river under a tree that would gave them shade. There was driftwood all around dried and ready for burning. Just behind the tent and a little higher up was a flat area where his father said he would build a tarpaper cabin. He also said that the nearest neighbors with children lived about 40 miles from us. It was a Mormon family, a man with two wives and four children: two girls and two boys about Benny Bob's age.

The man who worked with his father was waiting for them at the camp. His job was to help with making Desert Dew (Moonshine) that was sold in Las Vegas. He had a sleeping bag and a knapsack that was hung in the tree.

He would join them at the fire for mealtimes and eat with them. At night he would sit around the campfire telling stories and playing a guitar while everyone sang. During the day he worked carrying wood and water for making Desert Dew.

The still was located back from the river near where the car was parked. The dynamite Young Ben's father purchased in town was put in the cliff wall above the still and vats. If the still was ever

Ladies' Sand Box

discovered, the fuses were to be lighted and everyone was to run. Even Benny Bob was shown where the fuse ended, and where the matches were kept, so if no one else was able to light the fuses he could. Learning

No snakes in the water

how to protect the family and to be suspicious of strangers was something Ben learned at an early age. If you saw Benny Bob, it was because he wanted to get your attention. If you walked toward him, he was gone.

The very day they got to Base Camp, after the tent was up, Young Ben's father took him out to a sandbar next to camp. The really white sand was full of driftwood. His father was looking for Walking Sticks that would be just right for each of them.

His father finally found a stick that Young Ben could use. It was almost as long as he was tall. The stick was from a cottonwood tree, and it had a knob on one end. After he trimmed the

Fox pelts brought a good price.

stick, it was mostly straight and about one inch in diameter.

Young Ben really liked it and started using it as a stick horse. Later he even put a piece of rawhide string around the knob so it wouldn't get away.

His father's walking stick was about five feet long with a forked end on top. He even took his knife and made sure that the fork was trimmed smooth. His mother's walking stick was as long as his father's, but was straight with no knobs or forks.

About this time, Benny Bob saw his mother on another sandbar wading out into the river. He started to run to her, but his father grabbed him telling him that the sandbar was for ladies and girls only. Young Ben watched as she drove her walking stick into the sand and then hung her underpants on it. She then pulled up her dress before wading into the river. This was a real puzzle for Benny Bob. As long as they lived there, even when other women were in camp, they would visit the sandbar and go wading in the river. The girls laughed a lot, but never stayed in the water long.

Benny Bob soon found out that their walking sticks were not for walking at all. His father would use his with the forked end to catch snakes. First he would poke under rocks or bushes until the rattlesnake would strike out, then he would pin it down before grabbing it behind the head. Once he had it, he'd throw the snake into the river so it could swim down stream away from camp.

Benny Bob's walking stick was used to hit a bush or to poke under and move rocks around when he needed to drop his paints to do a do-do. The idea was not to shit on a snake because that might make it mad. Then Young Ben learned what the ladies were doing in the river, and on the sandbar. You don't have to worry about snakes in the river.

At night the men told stories around the campfire before going to sleep. The stories would be about how someone had gotten bitten by a diamond back rattlesnake or sidewinder.

Then they would tell stories about scorpions and lizards whose bite could kill you. One story was about a snake that would put its tail into its mouth and roll like a wheel faster than a person could run.

Today Benny Bob knows that all the stories were to teach him to keep his walking stick with him and how to use it. Ben still will not pee on a rock or shit in the open without first using a stick to dig a hole (mostly to check for snakes), and he always covers it when he's finished.

The Colorado River water temperature is always cold. Benny Bob was never allowed on

Tarpaper cabin after the flood

the sandbar or near the river at night. Every night the river seemed to rise six or more feet from rain or thunderstorms miles away. When the river came up, it was with a roar and a wall of water filled with all sorts of things the Colorado had found miles up stream — rocks, trees, and sometimes lumber. The river was the source of the camp's firewood and most of its building materials.

One night after Benny Bob fell asleep, his mother woke him and had him put on his shoes. Young Ben already had on shorts so he didn't have to get dressed. His father lit a lantern so everyone could see. His mother had on a slip-over dress, and his father had on pants but no shirt. You could hear a roaring noise, but it wasn't coming from the river.

His father pushed his mother out of the tent, grabbed Benny Bob up and ran toward the canyon wall. The noise was getting louder. They were climbing and Benny Bob noticed the water was up to his father's knees.

It wasn't raining, and the sky was full of stars. The stars gave enough light to see a little, and what he saw was water all around them except where they were climbing over the rocks to higher ground. Young Ben remembered the campfire stories and wanted to go back for his walking stick, but it was hanging in the tree with their food. Everything they owned, including the tent, was gone.

Suddenly, they could see his father's partner climbing to stand with them. He had pants on but no shirt or shoes. The river had taken everything else.

We stood there against the canyon wall until the sun came up, and by then the water was

Benny Bob, scout & camp guard, with Leroy Johnson at Base Camp

gone. There was no wreckage or even puddles of water left. It looked like no one had ever been there. His father told Benny Bob that the Colorado River had taken everything be-

Robert B. Games

cause somewhere down river someone needed it more than they did. He thought this must be true because that was how they found lumber or the firewood when they needed it.

Then mother told him to look at their Christmas tree. There was the tree that gave them shade. It was where they hung their sacks of food, and the things that they didn't want the mice or snakes to get into. There was Benny Bob's walking stick, the food sacks, the rifles, canteen, and even his father's partner's knapsack all hanging off the branches. It *was* just like a Christmas tree full of gifts for people who thought they had nothing left.

The water didn't come near the Desert Dew still, so they loaded up the car with Mountain Dew and went off to Las Vegas.

The Desert Dew business must have gotten better because they now lived in a tarpaper cabin. There was one window and a door. The floor was dirt, and there was a wood-burning stove for heat in the winter. Mother cooked outside, and father's partner got a new sleeping bag.

About that time, Benny Bob's father let Young Ben pick out his first rifle. It was a .22 and Young Ben had to practice until he could hit the eye of a snake. He was not allowed to kill anything with the rifle except snakes that he found with his walking stick.

Then he was given new work to help the family. After completing his chores, schoolwork, carrying water for the water barrel, and firewood every morning, he was free to do his new job. With the rifle slung on his back and his walking stick in hand, he'd report to his father at the still. His father would inspect the rifle and shells before instructing him to lead anyone he saw to the Base Camp. After his mother started talking to them he was to run and tell his father.

Young Ben was never allowed to talk to strangers or get near anyone. He didn't want to let any strangers see him often enough that they could follow him to camp. Benny Bob would climb the  hills, then circle around the still and where the car was parked all day. If his father saw him he'd get mad, and Young Ben would catch hell for it that evening. No one was to see him, not even his father. If the day went by without his father seeing him, then he'd be accused of not being on guard. Benny Bob finally solved the problem by letting himself be seen standing by a rock or on the trail once or twice a day just so his father would know he was on guard.

One day his father changed all of the dynamite and added more to the cliff above the still. He took the old sticks down to the river and put them on a sandbar. Then he told Young Ben to light the fuse just to see if he could do it. Benny Bob did and it was one big blast!

***

The family had been on the river for two years and his mother had been buying books in Las Vegas to teach Benny Bob reading, writing, and math. There was an old Army Fort about three miles from the tar-paper shack that had a cemetery beside it. His father told them that this was all going to be under water some day when they finished Boulder (Hoover) Dam.

Because of this, he decided that the graves had to be moved. Every Sunday they would go to the graveyard with his father and his partner. They would dig up the graves and bring the bones home. Mother would wash them, then place them on the roof of their tar-paper cabin to dry and bleach white in the sun.

His father would place the skull and bones of each soldier into separate sacks. They'd take them to Las Vegas when he delivered the Desert Dew. When they got to the cemetery at Las Vegas he would rebury them. No one ever saw them, and all the bodies were moved before the waters came.

The graves were so old there was no names visible on the stones. There were some officer's graves, but not many. You could tell which were officers because they would find a Masonic rings on their fingers. In one grave they found two bodies, but only one head.

There was a steamship that had been tied up along the riverbank. It was not very long maybe about thirty feet. The hull was full of mud up to about a foot from the top. The wood super structure and cabin of the boat were long gone. The old iron boiler sat in the center of the boat.

The current was very strong and was pushing against the boat. It looked like the boat had been headed upstream or tied up against a dock when it sank. There was no pier or dock there now, the Colorado must have taken them down river. The boat was now about ten feet from shore. There was a willow tree growing out of the bank of the river that went on a slant out over the river and boat.

Benny Bob had been on the river with his father when he used the same iron rings the soldiers had set in the canyon walls to help move their boat up river when it was used to haul freight. The canyon walls started about a mile up river and two miles down from where the boat was now sitting, however the current was on this side of the river, and it was fast.

One day while his father was digging up another grave so the bones could be moved, Young Ben decided to climb out over the old steam boat, and using a rope he let himself down to it. His plan was to use the rope to swing back and forth to reach the bank when he wanted to get back to shore.

Benny Bob took off his boots and left them with his walking stick on the bank, and then climbed the tree out over the steamboat. He had his rope over one shoulder. When he was over the boat he looked down and back to find a place to tie the rope. When he did this, he saw that he had crawled over one of the longest, biggest rattlesnakes he'd ever seen. The only reason the snake hadn't struck him was that it couldn't coil or turn with out falling into the water.

Since the snake couldn't turn around, it started coming toward Young Ben. Benny Bob started backing up and moving away from the snake. The tree started to bend toward the water. He was past the boat over the center of the current, and the snake was starting to slide toward him.

Right then Young Ben did what any good soldier would do, he jumped as far out and away from the snake as he could.

The tree snapped up, and Mr. Snake and Benny Bob hit the water about the same time. Young Ben started to dog paddle toward the shore, which was about thirty feet away. The current was fast and the shore was moving past and away from the old steam boat. That snake made a mistake as it started swimming down stream. It passed about two feet in front of Benny Bob, but he never stopped swimming at 90° to the current.

For awhile the shore was getting further away. It looked like a lost cause, but his mother had taught him well. She'd told him to just keep swimming and pay no attention to the riverbank. It's hard to do, but it works. Suddenly, the riverbank wasn't moving past as fast as it had been. Benny Bob was through the current. Finally the riverbank was getting closer and he found he could wade out.

All Young Ben had to do was walk up river for about a mile. He was soon back at the steamboat and his walking stick. He got back to the graveyard just as everyone was packing up to leave. He hadn't been missed. Benny Bob had already learned that if he did something his father didn't like, he'd get a whipping, and he was sure that his father wouldn't like hearing about him jumping into the river, so he didn't say anything about the snake.

They had been living on the river for over two years when their Mormon neighbor came to visit with his family. They had walked the forty miles with all four children. Young Ben's father made the farmer's two boys a walking stick, and the three boys pretended that they were stick horses to ride. They even branded them. It was a fun time, but Benny Bob was never able to show them the still or tell them about his work as a scout.

That night the boys hid close to the fire where the men were talking about some cowboys that had rustled about thirty cows and taken the farmer's milk cow when they passed his farm. He needed the milk for his family, and he had come to my father to ask for help getting the cow back.

The rustled herd of cows was being driven this way, and the farmer thought they would be driven to the river for water close to our camp.

My father asked the farmer how many cowboys there were and if they were armed. He was told there were three rustlers, and they were armed.

The men didn't want to kill the rustlers if they didn't have to; so, they decided to steal three cows while they were being watered. The farmer was to get two cows, and the camp would get one steer for food. The three boys crawled away from the fire and started to make plans for how they would outwit the rustlers. They were 9 to 11 years old and there were only three armed cowboys, so they figured it was an even fight.

The next day after breakfast, Benny Bob's father called a family meeting. The farmer told everyone what had happened and said that they were going to get the cow back or find a replacement for it. Then he told everyone they would have to help. Young Ben's father explained how it was going to be done and said that the herd of cows was expected the next day. Everyone was going to practice what they had to do until he was satisfied that the plan had a chance to work.

The three boys knew they didn't need any practice, and were sure they didn't need any help, but practice they did. After the meeting, the farmer asked for the Lord's help, and then the three boys were given their instructions. They had to help the women get ready. They were to get branches for brushing out the cow tracks, fill canteens, and help make up packets of jerky. They even had to help stash the water and jerky where they could get to them as they ran working the cows.

At noon the men returned and said they were ready. Everyone was told how the plan was to work once again. The herd had to pass through high brush to reach the river. It was so thick, that after drinking, the cows would have to be driven out of the brush by the cowboys along the riverbank down to the old Fort before continuing to wherever they were going.

The three boys were to go into the brush and use their walking sticks to drive three cows away from the herd. The plan was to drive them to a canyon that led up from the river into the mountains.

The women were to meet the boys at the edge of the brush. The women would continue to drive the cows up into the canyon while the boys swept away all the tracks so no one would see where the cows had gone. The men were to remain hidden in places, which they had picked, to watch the canyon and the ground where the brush stopped.

My father's partner had a .306 rifle with a scope, my father had the Winchester 30-30, and the farmer had my .22 rifle.

The cowboys (rustlers) looking for lost cows.

They said that they would stay hidden until the cowboys left with the herd. If the cowboys found or attacked the boys or women, the men would kill them. Otherwise, the cowboys would be left alone.

That afternoon, the young men practiced running through the brush to the river and on to the mouth of the canyon, while the men watched to be sure that they could see everyone. It took a while, but Benny Bob even learned when to

Benny Bob's father

duck branches that were big enough to knock a person down or a man off a horse.

The young men wore no hats and carried nothing but their walking sticks. The boys were brown from the sun and could run through the brush faster than a horse. There were canteens of water hidden near rocks and trees at different locations so they could drink and keep running.

The boys really had the most dangerous job, but after the practice, the men said they believed they could do it. Their mothers told them to run hard and not to say anything to each other. All the boys had to do was find three cows in the brush and drive them toward the mouth of the canyon.

They could hit the trees with their walking sticks, or hit the cows with them. It would sound like cows going through the brush. Nothing to it.

Well sometimes, even with practice, things don't go according to plan.

The next day, the farmer came to the camp and told us that the cows were in the brush and headed for the river. The three boys went into the brush and started walking with the cows. The cows had never seen anyone that wasn't on a horse, so they lowered their heads and charged. The boys hit them and then dodged behind a tree to get away. They didn't see any milk cows.

Benny Bob and his mother

The cowboys were trying to force the cows down the river to an open spot for drinking. The boys wanted to keep them in the brush, though, so they started to drive them toward the river. The cows finely smelled the water and started running toward it.

Now everyone was running. Benny Bob ran into one of the cowboy's horses, hitting it with his walking stick. The cowboy was so busy he must have thought it was a branch, because he just pushed the stick away and kept hitting at a running cow. When the cows got to the water the cowboys were busy keeping them from being pushed off the bank by other cows that wanted to drink.

The three boys just sat in the brush watching. After the first cows drank, they wandered back into the brush. The boys tried to pick three cows, but couldn't because the cows kept charging them. They finally found five cows, one with a calf, that they could drive toward the canyon. It was really hard work, but they finally got to the edge of the brush where the women and girls could help. The girls took over driving the cows while the three boys worked sweeping away the tracks as the cows were herded up the canyon.

The following day, the men had a meeting. The farmer would take two cows and the calf. He would start in an hour. He would leave a wife with the two boys to help with the camp's work until he could return. Young Ben's father said he would bring them home in his car in a week.

Benny Bob's father had the boys drive two of the other cows back down the canyon to the river. Then they had to sweep the ground removing all tracks to the canyon. He told everyone that the cowboys would be back looking for the missing cows, and he thought if they found two, they would think that the others couldn't be found.

He was right, two of the cowboys came back and spent the day looking. By evening, they took the two cows they found and headed back to the herd. I don't think they ever knew what happened or how lucky they were that they never saw the boys.

The next day, Benny Bob's father butchered the steer. There was more meat than the family could eat, so everyone helped make jerky. Young Ben's father put sheets of tin from the still out in the sun near the cabin while the women cut the meat into strips.

His father placed all of their pepper and salt into a bucket, then the women sprinkled it on the meat. The sun would cook it in a few hours and

Highway across the dessert

then it would be placed on rocks to cook for the rest of the day. Everyone ate and made jerky until all the meat was gone. The next day, Benny Bob's mother and father took his friends and their mother home. Young Ben stayed to guard the cabin and still.

Everyone went back to their regular work. Benny Bob returned to watching for strangers and studying schoolwork. A few days later, he heard a car in the distance heading towards the river. It would pass where the family car was parked.

Eventually, he could see it. It was a big touring car, much bigger than the Model A Ford. It stopped, and two men would get out and look for tracks at each wash they came to. They were looking for the Ford's parking place. If they kept on coming, they would soon find the wash with their car in it.

Young Ben ran across the trail they were on so he could be seen by the men in the car. The car stopped and the men got out. Everyone stood looking at each other. They were looking at a skinny nine-year-old (almost ten) wearing a wide brim hat, brown shirt, big shoes with tire soles,

*Desert Dew Company —
The best Dew in Las Vegas, 1933*

and a rifle over his shoulder carrying a walking stick.

He was looking at two black men wearing blue suits. One was wearing black and white shoes, and the other had on black shoes. They each weighed over two hundred pounds and must have been more than six feet tall. They were a hundred feet from Benny Bob.

They were close enough, but if they started to get back in to their car Young Ben would let them get closer. He just stood there and let them walk until they were within fifty feet of him before he turned and ran. He got a distance away, then stopped to see if they had followed. They had, so he waited until they got closer then he ran to where the trail turned toward the base camp.

They started to follow again, and he ran ahead, but had to stop fast because right in the middle of the trail was one big rattlesnake. He was coiled and mad, so Benny Bob gave him the trail and darted up and around him before he stopped again. Suddenly, there was a lot of cursing before two shots rang out. They sounded loud, so he knew that the two strangers were both armed, and not with small guns.

He waited until they came out of the brush, then ran toward the cabin and his mother. She was watching while standing beside the woodpile with an ax as if she had been chopping wood. Benny Bob kept right on going, picking up steam and running fast. He was on his way to

Lighting the fuse — the end

the still where is father and his father's partner were working.

As Young Ben came up the wash, they saw him, and he turned around, still running, and headed back the way he came. His father poured water on the fire, and both men grabbed their rifles. They were on their way to camp.

As Young Ben got closer, he stopped and looked out between the boulders. There were the two black men talking to his mother. She was standing about 30 feet from the strangers beside the woodpile, still holding the ax.

Benny Bob circled around and showed himself. He was standing just off the trail that led to their car. This time he was holding his rifle and his walking stick was lying on the ground beside him. Young Ben was a hundred feet back from the trail, just watching.

About this time his father appeared carrying his 30-30 Winchester. He was in the mouth of the wash about 50 feet from them. He spoke to the two men, but Young Ben couldn't hear what was said. No one was afraid because his father's partner was nowhere to be seen. All the talk was to give him time to get in position with the 306-scope rifle. Benny Bob wasn't worried, and his mother didn't seem to be either. Those dudes just stood there and acted like they wanted to be somewhere else.

After they finally left, his father held a family meeting. His partner joined the meeting; so, Young Ben knew it was an important one. He got to sit next to his mother and listen because he had been the one who sounded the alarm and then carried the word. His father reported that he had noticed someone had tried to follow their car back to the river on their last two trips to Las Vegas. He also said he thought it was strange that those dudes acted so scarred.

Everyone was sitting beside the campfire as they talked about how those two men acted, then Young Ben's father started to laugh. He kept pointing to the cabin, but

Benny Bob, water boy

no one could see anything. Then he told us to look at the roof. There were two skeleton heads above the door and bones laying on the roof waiting to go to Las Vegas. That sight must've really shook up the visitors. Especially after they'd seen the rattlesnake guarding the trail. The skulls with the bones over the cabin door were probably the perfect, scary finishing touch!

Young Ben's father and his partner decided that these men would be back with a lot more of their friends because the moonshine business was getting too big for them to forget about our Desert Dew Plant. His mother agreed, so Benny Bob helped her pack and carry everything to the car. They even took the last of the soldier's bones with them to bury when they got to Las Vegas. That way the bones would be where they belonged — with the other soldiers.

As they were carrying the bones to the car, they heard the explosion as the dynamite erased the Desert Dew Factory. They didn't even carry any samples of moonshine with them. Benny Bob left his walking stick hanging in the tree next to the cabin just in case he needed it again some day.

***

Upon arrival in Las Vegas, they moved into a tourist cabin at the El Rancho Vegas, and Benny Bob was given a job bringing a herd of dairy cows in from the range for milking twice a day. In 1933, the ranch was a cattle, dairy, and pig farm. El Rancho Vegas even had a contract to pick up the garbage in Las Vegas to feed their pigs. It was one of the largest pig farms in Nevada.

Young Ben's mother enrolled him in the Vegas City Grade School. The only thing Young Ben remembers about this school was how all the teachers chased him. He had never seen a fire alarm switch before. When Young Ben pulled the fire alarm handle, he once again proved to his mother, as well as every teacher in the school, that he could outrun them all. His mother was smarter than the others, and she told them not to try to catch him. She would catch him when he got back to the ranch. She knew those teachers never had a chance.

***

During a large part of the time while Benny Bob was growing up, he did chores and helped his father. His father had three jobs and they all involved the Colorado River and water. One was Prospecting for gold, another was making Desert Dew, and the third was running a pack train for the U.S. Geological Survey Team working on Boulder (Hoover) Dam.

Benny Bob thought of these chores as work because he carried pails of water from the river and emptied them into wooden barrels. The water then sat overnight so the silt could settle to the bottom.

The following day, his father could use the water in his work, and then Ben had to fill them again. Young Ben must admit that herding cows for the El Rancho Vegas, and riding a burro on his father's packtrain was fun. Even currying a hot horse, or being bitten by a burro was just part of the job. The thing he remembers most is carrying all those buckets of water. Even today, this is not his idea of a fun thing to do.

Author's Note:

When I was flying as an Army Helicopter Aircraft Commander in Vietnam, I remembered how dangerous a ten-year-old soldier can be. Sometimes after a Firefight at an Army LZ I would be asked to take wounded children to a MASH Unit for treatment. I always had them strip-searched, then seated them between two Vietnamese soldiers where they could not talk to each other. I never had a problem, but other companies lost helicopters and crews when children came aboard carrying live hand grenades.

I remembered that there was no fear when we three boys were running through the brush with armed rustlers, cows crazy with thirst, and rattlesnakes. Even with the cowboys trying to turn the cows, we followed our instructions and were able to keep the cows running towards the river. Our ages were nine to eleven, so I was sure that the Vietnamese child soldiers were like us. They had a cause, and right or wrong, it's hard to stop a determined soldier with no fear. **That's a FACT.**

DYNAMITE

Ben R. Games, PhD

1931

To understand why someone would pick a profession where violence was only seconds away and death was a constant possibility it's necessary to know about the person's childhood. **That's a FACT.**

USG Construction Crew

Adventures of Benny Bob

In the spring of 1930 during the Great Depression, Benny Bob's father took his family on his work site with a construction gang for the Boulder (Hover) Dam Project in Nevada. His father worked as a blacksmith for the construction crew that was erecting river Gage Wells above and below the dam along the mighty Colorado River.

The work gang consisted of 12 men who moved to a new construction site every three months. Benny Bob's mother and two other crew members' wives worked in the mess hall preparing meals.

They established a work camp on the banks of the Colorado River in Willow Beach, Arizona. It was down river from the construction of Hoover Dam, and a little over a mile below the new Gage Well site. In springtime along the river the weather was cold in the morning

Benny Bob with the toddlers

Work gang getting ready to cross river

and over a hundred degrees by 1500 hours when work ceased for the day. When the men returned down river from the work site, they had to clean and fill four 55-gallon water barrels each day for the camp's use.

The river was so swift that the water was brown form the dirt it picked up on the way to the Gulf of California. The workmen didn't like to carry buckets of water any more than Benny Bob, but they made a deal with him. Every man paid him 10 cents a day to fill the barrels with muddy river water so it could settle overnight and provide clean water for drinking and cooking.

Each of the women in the camp had a child; two were just toddlers. At that time, cowboys made a dollar a day working on a ranch, but

Mess hall and cooks

Young Ben was making $1.20 per day keeping the camp's water barrels full.

Carrying all that water taught Benny Bob two things he's never forgotten: Learn how to make money without carrying water all day, and it's great to have money to spend when you go to Kingman, AZ.

Of the 12 men working on the Gage Well crew, only three had families with them, and they lived in their own tents down near the river. The base camp had two large government tents. One

Camp cooks

was the barracks or bunkhouse where the single men slept, and the other was the mess tent which also acted as a reading room and lounge for the camp.

Because it was cold at night the mess tent had a wood-burning stove just inside and to the right next to the tent's only door. The floor was made of wood raised about two feet above the ground, and it had four foot high wooden sides. The tent's canvas sides could be raised at noon to help cool the air for the evening meal which was served around 1600 hours. There was no noon meal served in the mess tent because the work gang was a mile up river at the job site. The women would make a lunch

Benny Bob with mother and father on the way to gage well

Benny Bob & Pot Licker

out of bread they'd baked, pressed canned meat, iced tea, and beans. They would send it with the men when they left in the morning.

In the mess hall the men were fed first, and after they had finished, the women and children would eat. Because Benny Bob's job was keeping the camp supplied with water and the water barrels clean, he was allowed to eat with the men.

There was no latrine because the camp was only used for about three months. Everyone used the river or the desert. The only rule posted on the mess hall bulletin board was: if you use the desert, cover your shit. I never saw any toilet paper, but there were two or three Sears and Roebuck Catalogs available.

All of the men got three days off every two weeks so they could go into Kingman. Someone had to stay in camp during these times, so the married families took turns.

There was only one small out building built completely out of wood and located in sight of the mess tent. It was covered with about a foot of dirt, and its only door was kept padlocked. No one was allowed in or near it except the men who worked blasting the trail and rocks above the catwalk to the Gage Well. It was the work gang's powder magazine, and was used to store six or more cases of dynamite with fuses and caps.

Every morning the Powder Monkeys (the men who handled the explosives) would take out the number of sticks of dynamite, caps, and fuses they needed for the day, and take them up to where they were blasting a trail to the site of the gage well. No one would be returning to the camp site until it was time to put fire in the hole (blast the rock).

Benny Bob visiting father at the blacksmith. Early morning just after the sun came up.

Whenever he got the chance, Young Ben watched the Powder Monkeys as they prepared the fuses and put them into the sticks of dynamite. First they cut off the length of fuse adjusted to the time needed, then they put a blasting cap on the fuse by clenching it in their teeth. They would use a wooden stick to make a hole in a stick of dynamite and then place the fuse.

Every day at 1500 when they were blasting, the men would come down the trail and just be entering camp when the explosions occurred. They would all stop and count the blasts. If all the sticks had gone off, everyone would be laughing as they started cleaning up for the evening meal. If there was a blast short, everyone just held their breath.

Most of the time when all the dynamite didn't explode it was due to fuse length or a slow burning fuse, and the explosion was just late. There was only one time the blast didn't occur. The next morning two of the powder monkeys left early carrying tennis shoes and gloves. No one ate breakfast. They just stood around waiting, not even talking. Even when the blast came, they still didn't go into the mess tent for breakfast. Finally when the two powder monkeys appeared on the trail, everyone started laughing and talking at the same time.

Benny Bob decided that Powder Monkey must be a fun job, so he took to walking over to the powder magazine and just looking around. He never got close enough to get yelled at.

One day the women wanted to have fish for dinner. One of the Powder Monkeys opened the powder shed and cut a six-inch fuse crimped on a cap then placed it in a stick of dynamite. Everyone followed him down to the river to an eddy where the water was calm. He tied a rock to the dynamite stick, lit the fuse, and threw it into the water.

When it went off the water rose straight up into the air and fish were floating all around on top of the water. There was more than enough fish for everyone.

***

The problem with storing dynamite is you have to keep it cool and dry. The wooden cases were lined on the inside with heavy waxed paper like the kind on the dynamite sticks. When a case was empty, the men working with it would burn the paper and the box in the mess-hall heating stove.

One day Ben found an old broom handle that his mother had put outside of the mess hall door for the men to cut up for firewood. Young Ben was bored and had nothing to do except carry water, so he cut off a length of the handle to resemble a stick of dynamite. He waited, and sure enough a day later there was an empty case. He offered to carry it to the mess hall for burning, and it was given to him.

Off he went with the case. As he walked across the campground, Benny Bob was able to get a piece of the waxed paper into his pocket without anyone noticing. Now all he needed was a length of fuse.

Everyday he watched and waited trying to find a piece of fuse. A week went by before the women wanted fish for another meal. This time, Young Ben asked if he could cut the fuses for the dynamite sticks. One of the Powder Monkeys showed him how and let him cut one about six inches long. Somehow no one noticed that he cut two pieces of fuse. They also didn't see one go into his pocket. Fuses are not dangerous, so no one thought about it.

Benny Bob had no way to drill a hole in the wood for the fuse, so he put the fuse next to the wood and wrapped both with waxed paper. Then he crimped the paper tight around the fuse and at the end of the stick. It looked just like a stick of dynamite if he held his hand around the fuse end of the stick. Now came the test.

The next morning, the men were eating breakfast, and the women were serving them. It was a cold morning, and the fire in the heating

Adventures of Benny Bob

Benny Bob and his father

stove was burning, giving off warm waves of air. To feed the stove, you could lift open the door in the front, or remove a round plate from the top where a coffee pot was sitting.

That morning, Ben's mother and the other ladies had left before daylight to prepare breakfast. His father went to make the fire in the mess tent and to put firewood in the box next to the stove.

Benny Bob waited until all the work gang started to eat before entering the mess tent carrying his fake dynamite stick. As he entered, someone called out for him to close the door. As he closed it, Young Ben turned around so all could see what he was holding in his right hand. Someone yelled that it was dynamite and told him to get rid of it! Benny Bob turned quick as a flash, opened the stove door with his left hand and threw in the fake stick of dynamite.

One of the ladies was at the cooking stove making pancakes, and one was pouring coffee while his mother had dirty dishes heading for a tub where they could be washed. Everything happened faster than he could keep track of.

The only thing Young Ben saw was his mother's eyes as she tore through the workmen who were trying to get out of the tent. She was moving fast, jumping to clear the turned over table and benches to try to get him.

She knew her son, and it wasn't love Benny Bob saw in her eyes — she was an angry mother trying to catch her naughty son. He turned and dove out the door, moving fast up the trail toward the work site. His father wasn't far behind his mother, but had lost ground when he stopped for a willow switch.

Some of the men had dived over the mess tent walls bringing down the tent. Someone had knocked over the gallon coffee pot and food was everywhere. Benny Bob was dressed in shorts and a shirt but no shoes. He was moving fast up the trail, but his father knew that the trail would end a mile upstream, 50 feet along a sheer cliff, and about thirty feet above the Colorado River.

Trail from camp to river gage well

When the work crews finished the day before, they had added enough iron rods for another hundred feet of wooden planks along the cliff.

His parents may have known their son, but must have forgotten that they had trained him to always plan for the unexpected. It is true he never expected to run for his life, but, just in case, for the last week he had been practicing diving into the Colorado River just below and out of sight of the workmen in a make believe getaway.

Today, even barefooted running over the rocky trail, he was keeping ahead of his mother. It's also true his mother and father had slowed down because they were sure he would have to stop at the end of the trail. They were about fifty feet behind him when the trail ran out and the catwalk began. As Young Ben ran out onto the catwalk, they stopped and watched. He didn't hesitate but ran to the end and jumped from one iron rod to another before turning with a push off the cliff; making a 20-foot dive into the river.

It happened just like he'd practiced the past five times he had tried it. The river was carrying him so fast that by the time he passed his mother she had already turned and started back to camp. Benny Bob didn't wave, but he could see all the workmen scattered along the trail on their way to work and all of them were waving as he floated past.

The river current was very fast near the cliff, but moved across toward the center and then to the opposite side of the river across form the camp. It was important to time everything right to avoid missing the camp area. First he needed to find a wooden plank to hang on to so he wouldn't be tired. Next, he had to watch for

Pier in front of the work camp

A desert mushroom

a piece of cloth he had tide to a willow near the river's edge that told him the camp was around the next bend.

During the building of Hoover Dam, the workmen were always dropping wood into the river. There was so much that all of the wood in the building of the camp came from the river. What the camp didn't need was pushed back into the river for the people down stream.

The foreman had paid Benny Bob five cents for planks that could be used for a catwalk. There was no reason to miss another opportunity to make a nickel since he was already in the water. Sure enough, a long plank floated by and Young Ben started to work it toward the position where it could be pushed out of the current and maneuvered to camp.

By the time he arrived with his prize, his mother was standing on the bank to help him pull the plank ashore. All she said was to get up to the mess-tent because they needed help with the breakfast and lunch that needed to be delivered to the workmen.

The ladies had pulled the tent off the floor and laid it against the wall. The benches and table were set back up waiting for the men to put the tent in place when they returned to camp. Because they hadn't taken their lunch with them that morning, two of the workmen came down the trail to pick up the food. This time the ladies had fixed a lunch and breakfast together with twice the amount of food. His mother had baked two apple pies the day before and had included them in the lunch.

Benny Bob was not allowed to eat with the men for the rest of the time during construction of the gage well. The ladies were not nice to him either, but they were afraid of his mother so they didn't say too much. His father was kidded, and the men made jokes about missing breakfast until his father offered to fight them one at a time or all at once. The foreman inspected the timber that Benny Bob brought ashore and declared it was a twenty-five cent plank.

Author's Note:

Ben never forgot about how his mother and father taught him to prepare for the unexpected. It saved him from a sure spanking.

During his military flying there was never a mission or situation that he hadn't practiced and planned for. When he was shot down in combat, though, he hadn't planned for that. He had, however, planned different escapes and how to get home just in case. It happened in Vietnam and the plan worked, but not exactly according to script.

Benny Bob, 1934. Home at Lee's Ferry, Arizona

NAVAHO CLIFF HIEROGLYPHICS

1934

In the winter of 1934, Benny Bob and his parents lived in a log cabin that had a sod roof, dirt floors, and a fireplace. It was situated just below the cliff facing the Colorado River as far upstream as one could walk from Lee's Ferry, Arizona. He attended the third grade in a one-room schoolhouse with nine other children from grades one through eight.

There was a dirt road leading into the village that passed three Navajo hogans before it crossed in front of the schoolhouse. The school building was painted white and had a bell for calling the children when classes started.

The road continued on and turned to the right after passing the bottom of a steep slope of shale red rock that went up to near the beginning of a plateau. The plateau was full of small caves and extended as far as the eye could see. After making the ninety-degree turn, the road passed in front of three more homes before it found a place to ford the creek that followed a canyon on its way to the mighty Colorado River. There was no bridge, and after fording the creek it continued on to its end at a fresh water spring and the log cabin home of Benny Bob.

Halfway from the creek to the mouth of the canyon where the Colorado River came out between high canyon walls, the road passed two other houses made of shale rock with sod roofs. For the next quarter mile, the road ran straight with the mighty river on the right and a flat washed out area that led up to the base of a high cliff on the left.

On the side of the road, away from the river, there were five mammoth hydraulic pumps that

Class of 1934—Grade 1 thru 8, Lee's Ferry

looked like spaceships to a ten year old with an imagination. There were also three large steel pipes with nozzles on swivel platforms that looked like weapons of some sort. This was all that remained of a hydraulic gold mining operation that existed long before Lee's Ferry, Arizona became a small Mormon-farming village.

The distance from the log cabin to the schoolhouse was about three miles, and each school morning, Benny Bob's mother would get him up before daylight and start him walking down the road. He was always dressed in breaches, high top boots, leather jacket, and carried a walking stick. Because of the high cliff behind the log cabin, the sun didn't peek over until about 0900 hours.

By the time he reached the open area in front of the old hydraulic mining operation, it was just starting to get light. With the early morning light and the shadows from the high cliffs, the hydraulic pumps became spaceships, the water nozzles became weapons, and his walking stick became a Zorro-knife. Every morning while walking to school, Benny Bob ran that quarter of a mile to pass those spaceships and whatever alien space creature that might want to have him for breakfast. A young man's imagination is a wonderful thing.

At night, Benny Bob's mother would point up at the clear Arizona night sky and show her son shooting stars. She told him that they weren't really stars. They were rocks or ice from passing comets. That night he would dream that they were ice crystals from flying saucers or spaceships coming to Lee's Ferry, Arizona. Even 70 years after those daily runs and nightly dreams, the author can remember them as if they were only yesterday.

Benny Bob was in the third grade with one other boy. Although Lee's Ferry school included grades one through eight, there were only 10 students in the school.

There was no money used in the village, only watermelons that were traded to the Indians in the Navaho Reservation on the other side of the Colorado River. The state of Arizona paid $10 a month for someone to sweep the floors of the school, carry wood for the stove, and wash the windows. Cleave La Baron and the other farmers acting as the school board agreed to allow each student to do the school chores for one month so all the children could have enough money for shoes and proper clothing to attend classes.

Cooling off after a day's work

There were 10 children in the school, so the school board extended the school year to ten months. Benny Bob got to attended the third grade for 10 months.

The Principal, and only teacher, had studied Navaho history in college and moved west to be near the Navaho Reservation. On Friday afternoons, she would teach all classes about the Indians who lived across the river. If the students worked hard and behaved all week, she would tell them a story of the Navaho Nation. At the same time, she would draw hieroglyphic cliff drawings that told the story of the Indians on the blackboard — just like they would have drawn or carved them in the rocks.

On Saturdays, Benny Bob and his friends would go up to the base of a cliff where there were real Indiana hieroglyphic writings. They would carve their story in the cliff using the same stone tools the Indians had used hundreds of years ago. Today, visitors to the national park can see these true Navaho stores carved in the cliff. They are true historical records of the Navaho Nation as told by their medicine men, but not all of them were written by Indians.

The water wagon at Lee's Ferry

MOTHER'S RING

by Ben R. Games, PhD

At 0900 hours, the sun would start peeking over the cliff looking down upon our log cabin. The morning would be cold and the sky clear blue. The cabin was up the river at the beginning of Marble Canyon just below the cliffs where the Colorado River came roaring out. From the cabin, a person could look across the river into Navajo Indian country.

The cabin had first been used as the ferry house for crossing the Colorado River at Lee's Ferry, Arizona. With one room, a stone fireplace, sod roof, and dirt floor, it was the finest house in the canyon. In February 1934, we added a stone lean-to for a bedroom and a sun porch. All had sod roofs and dirt floors. My father built a Dutch oven outside by the porch where my mother did all of the cooking and baking for the family.

The fireplace was for heat since the high cliffs kept the sun from warming the cabin until late morning. There was a fresh water spring about 500 feet from the cabin. The outhouse was near the front and only door. All I can remember about the outhouse was that there was no door or seat. My father had found a branch of a tree with no bark that had floated down the river, and we used that to sit on.

We had no toilet paper, but we had a Sears and Roebuck Catalog with a lot of pictures to

Home along the Colorado River

look at. The catalog had so many pages, it would last our family almost a year, pretty much until the next catalog was received in the mail.

To take a bath everyone went swimming. My mother always took soap with her so I tried to swim as far away as possible. In those days I saw no reason to mix soap with water while swimming. I also remember that the water was very cold.

My mother worked for the US Weather Bureau, and my father worked for the US Geological Survey on the Boulder Dam Project in Arizona and Nevada. From Lee's Ferry he took a boat up the river, carrying spring water and supplies to the Survey Gangs in their camps. My mother went across the river to read the gauge well that measured the rise and fall of the river every other day.

Whenever she went across the river I went with her to help row because the river was so swift that when we rowed across the boat ended up over a mile down stream. I would pull it back up the river, then help my mother read the water gauges and clean the silt from the well. When we returned to our side of the river, the boat again ended up over a mile down stream, and we would pull it back up to the cabin.

I was only 8 years old, and one of my jobs was to ride a one-horse water wagon once a day from the spring to Lee's Ferry, a Mormon village. I would walk the three miles from our cabin to the one-room schoolhouse where the water wagon was parked, then go to Cleve LaBaron's first wife's house and catch the horse that Cleve wasn't using. I'd hitch it to the water wagon, drive to the spring, fill up and return to the village, then walk home again.

The water in the creek that I had to ford to get there was always wide and over ankle deep, so I had to take off my boots and wade across. When you only get one pair of boots a year, they were always too big in the spring and to short in the fall.

On a Saturday in February, my mother looked up from her work sprinkling the floors with water (she had to wet down the floors every day to keep them from drying up and getting dusty) and saw two Indians standing on the bank of the river across from our cabin watching us. Now we knew about the Navajo Indians because they had three of their hogans about a block from the schoolhouse. They stayed in them when they visited Lee's Ferry to trade for watermelons.

My mother called for me to get the boat ready. We rowed across the mighty Colorado River to pick them up. They just stood there and watched as we came over. When we pulled the boat back up the river, they got in and sat in the stern. I pulled on one oar and my mother pulled on the other, rowing them to our side of the river. I remember that they wore hats and had blankets over their shoulders to keep warm. I never saw any bags or items that they may have been carrying.

They never spoke to us, just got in the boat, and waited to get across the river. They were trading silver and petrified wood in the village, but only with the men. On their way down to the river, they had walked through a petrified forest of trees. I'd been there many times, but the logs were to big to carry, and we had no use for whole trees that had turned to stone.

Three days later, when my mother got up to make breakfast, there were the two Indians sitting under our covered porch saying nothing;

just waiting. My mother told me to get the boat ready for a dawn trip across the river.

The Indians never spoke to my mother, but one told me to help carry one of the sacks they had. I didn't even answer him. I just picked up the oars, and started walking to the boat with my mother. When we got there, we stood and waited until they had their sacks loaded, then took them back across the river once again.

When we got home, my mother found the ring they had placed on the bench where they had been sitting. It was a silver band with a setting made out of petrified wood taken from the trees across the Colorado River from our log cabin. It was size 7, the polished petrified wood setting was 3/4" long by 1/2" wide with 20 silver balls around the wood. It was not signed but there are construction marks on the silver.

After that day, the Indians would stand by the riverbank when they wanted a boat ride to our side. Lee's Ferry was back in business. My mother found jewelry on the same bench after every crossing. They never spoke to her, but sometimes they told me what they wanted, and I would tell her.

***

One time while my mother was checking the fall and rise of the river in the gauge well, she slipped and fell. The well had a hook where she hung the float while she was cleaning the silt from the bottom. When she fell, her ring caught on the hook and tore into her left finger. The bone stopped the ring, and held her weight until I could get under her. I lifted to help get her off the hook, and she was able to climb out of the well.

Then, holding pressure on the finger with her right hand to slow the bleeding, we headed back to the boat. I grew up fast that day as mother leaned on me while we walked up stream for at least a mile to where the boat was moored. She sat in the stern, and I rowed the boat back across the river. With my small size, it took twice the time and distance to make the crossing. Then we had to walk back up the river to our cabin.

I left the boat where we had landed, and went to the village for help. Cleve came and bandaged her hand, but didn't want to remove the finger because he thought that a doctor could save it. There were no cars in Lee's Ferry, but the US mailman drove a Ford Model A pickup truck and brought the mail once a week. He was due the following day, so Cleve told me that he would ask him to take mother to a doctor in Page, Arizona. I had to stay home to check the weather station and gauge well, besides there was no room for me in the truck.

She was very lucky because gangrene had set in by the time she got to the doctor, but they were able to save her finger. The mailman brought her back to Lee's Ferry after two weeks. Cleve paid the doctor and mailman with watermelons because no one in the village had money.

My father repaid Cleve by helping the farmers build a dam across the creek that would irrigate their crops when he got back from up river.

I must admit that I was scared when she was hurt, but was more disappointed that no Indians came while she was gone. I was hoping that I would get a ring like my mother did.

My mother, Mary Opal Florence (Tate) Games, (Betty Jo) gave this ring to Helen Marie (Amsden) Games in June of 1943, when we got married. Helen has since given this ring to her granddaughter, Margo Marie Games, in February of 2001.

The pictures of our home at Lee's Ferry were taken by mother with a Kodac Box Camera. My father was away for weeks at a time working with the US Geological Survey Teams on the Boulder Dam (Hoover Dam) project.

THE PIGS STRATAGEM

by Elizabeth M. Baker

1900

A dog and a pig were on board a ship. They were very good friends generally, and they always ate their food off the same dish. The only thing they quarreled about was their lodging.

There was a nice comfortable kennel built for two, but sometimes the dog would get in the kennel first. Then he would bark, show his teeth, and frighten the pig away. Other times the pig would get in the kennel first, and the dog could not make it get out.

The only thing the dog could do to get revenge was wait until after the next meal and run so it got in the kennel first. The dog was a faster runner on the slippery ship's deck and most nights the pig had to sleep on the open.

One dark stormy evening when the ship was rolling rather heavily, the pig was slipping and tumbling about on the deck. When it got to the kennel it found the dog curled in the doorway fast asleep.

With the wind blowing rain and the sea across the wet slippery deck it was no place for a man or beast to sleep, so the clever pig went and got the tin plate they ate from. Taking it a little ways from the door of the kennel, he then made sounds like he was eating.

He was noisy and it woke the dog. The dog did not like the pig to get all the meat, so out of the kennel the dog ran. He pushed the pig to one side, and then put his muzzle into the empty plate. While the dog was checking to see if any food had fallen out of the dish, the pig rushed into the kennel and lay down at the rear leaving room for the dog to sleep in the doorway.

With the dog in its favorite spot blocking the doorway, both were happy. The cold rain couldn't get passed the dog, and the pig was dry and warm in the back of the kennel.

***

Miss Elizabeth M. Baker, BS, was a US Army Captain Nurse in the Spanish American War. She was also Benny Bob's grandmother.

Everyone Has a Story

Benny Bob is now the chief member of the "Games Clan," and believes that everyone has a story to tell. Keeping a journal or diary will document the story and become the building blocks needed for a window that looks into the future. What has happened in the past can happen again unless a change in the pattern of things is made. Some have tried to change history by rewriting it, but this never works. History must be lived, and today is tomorrow's history.

When Ben wrote his autobiography at the request of the US Army Historical Library he found that it would take more than two or more books to tell his complete story. One book tells about Benny Bob joining the US Army and becoming a pilot during WW II and the Korean War. Another is about military missions and flying in the Detroit Riots and Vietnam. Many stories are about adventures with Helen, who decided to help him while she was raising their family. Ben is not writing history but only what he did in it.

Helen, his wife, has encouraged him to continue writing his autobiography even if it sometimes differs a little from how she remembers it. Ben has agreed to do this, but he writes it as a semi-biography with each adventure as a separate short story. When all of the stories are put together, they form the autobiography of the man born in Elkhart, Indiana on 5 May, 1924. The historical section of each story includes pictures and documents related to the story. This way a reader can judge for himself if any part is conjecture.

When Ben refers to his family, he is including the animals who share the Games' home and adventures. Helen's service dog, Montana, travels with them, and they avoid countries where dogs are not welcome.

A GRANDFATHER'S PRAYER

Last night I prayed:

Lord, please give me the wisdom to help my grandson become a man. Please God show me the way; help me understand my grandson's problems; help me feel what he is feeling; help me become wise so that I may guide my grandson on the path he must take while learning how to be a member of your family. I ask these things in the name of your son Jesus Christ, Amen.

This morning when I looked into the mirror while shaving, the reflection looking back at me was not an old man with white hair and wrinkled skin but the face of my grandson. When I winked, the reflection winked. I put my hand on my face, and it was my grandson's hand in the mirror. Then I knew that every father who looks into a mirror can see his son's face, and every grandfather can see his son and grandson's reflection.

The reflection in the mirror showed me that my grandson will walk in his father's shoes someday, and that he may also walk on the path grandfather has taken. If he looks down the path, he will see his father working. If he looks further ahead, he will see an old man also helping to clear the path, and he will know that his grandfather is leading the way.

To feel and understand my grandson's problems, I must remember how I felt when I was fifteen. Many times I made mistakes, and it was never easy. Now I can help by removing some of the roadblocks that my grandson will face. If I am successful I will have helped him a little.

He will still be a free agent, though, and must make his own decisions. Nothing can keep me from the hurt that I will feel when he takes a wrong step, because I will always be his grandfather. The path my grandson must follow can be long and rough. It will have many forks and bends before he can look ahead to see his father working to clear and smooth the way. Perhaps he may look back and see another young man starting his journey upon the same road. Then he will have the opportunity to work helping his son learn to find his way along life's path.

THE GUARDIAN ANGEL

Ben R. Games, PhD

A young boy watched the birds fly and thought, "Why can't I?"

Then in Sunday School he learned that Angels fly and thought, "Why can't I?"

The young man and woman holding hands stood looking up at the clouds in the sky and the woman said, "Why don't we fly?"

Now the Lord has a plan for all his children. He looked down and saw that they were getting ahead of the plan. If something wasn't done there would be a traffic jam at the Pearly Gates. He called the Archangel Michael and told him to think of ways to help the plan.

The Archangel formed a committee of Angels and told them that the Head Man had said to do something. They decided that every pilot must have a Guardian Angel to watch over him or her to see that they did not show up at the Pearly Gates before their time.

Then the Archangel went back to the Lord. He told him about the Committee and their idea. Then he asked the Lord which Angel to assign to the task. The Lord sighed and looked again. There were so many trying to fly that one Angel would never do. The Lord said, "These are my Children so assign all the Angels who watch over the children to take turns watching over pilots."

So it came to pass that every pilot was assigned a Guardian Angel to help see that he didn't get into heaven before his time.

Dedicated to The Guardian Angel of USAFA
Rickenbacker Class 2004

Mathew A. Knight, Cadet — 1982-2001

Endurance

by Mathew A. Knight, (author at age 16)

Never give up,
No matter who tells you it's okay,
You must keep pressing on,
Never be content to stay.
Push! Push! And dig down deep within,
Try your hardest, and even if you fall,
You know that you've done more than most;
You've given it your all.
All of the effort, which sometimes seems for nothing,
Those hard days you've been struggling to understand,
Don't do it for anyone but yourself,
Finish the flight, do your best, be absolutely all that you can.
When you receive discouragement,
Or trials to your faith,
The future seems uncertain,
And all life seems a waste.
Just try to keep on believing,
Keep on pressing on,
For in the end,
You're only accountable to one:
YOURSELF.

Forward, Shangri-la Vietnam

The poem "Shangri-la Vietnam" was written by Ben R. Games, PhD, Major, CW-4, TCNA-6, the man from Elkhart, IN, and dedicated to the Vietnam Helicopters Pilot Association (VHPA). It was first published by Bookman Publishing, LLC in Little Big BOOKS, subtitled *Poems and Stuff* in 2004.

In 1969/70, the author flew Chinook CH-47 helicopters for the 1st Cavalry Division in Vietnam as a Warrant Officer Army Aviator. His military flying career started with USA Pilot Class 43K and continued until his retirement in January 1978. He flew bombers and night fighters during WW II and jet fighters during the Korean period.

His flight records show 737 combat flight hours. He was awarded the Distinguished Flying Cross, Bronze Star, 13 Air Medals, 2 Legion of Merit, 2 Medal for Valor, and the Army Commendation Medal.

The author is married to Helen M. Games (Amsden) of Goshen, Indiana, who was the 86th woman in the world to fly a helicopter. They have two sons, Ben Jr. (Bud) and Jon, who are also licensed pilots.

During WW II, Helen flew with Ben in Army Trainers and occasionally in bombers as his copilot. In Okinawa, she once flew a mission as his RO in an F-82G fighter. In Vietnam, she lived on a Thai firebase named Bearcat and has flown with him in his Chinook helicopter named "City of Elkhart."

Ben Jr. served eight years in the Navy with one year ashore in Da Nang, Vietnam. At the age of 15, Jon completed combat training at Fort Rucker, AL, during his summer vacation and spent his Christmas vacation in Vietnam. Besides visiting his parents on Bearcat, he flew as a pilot in a UH-1 Slick helicopter before returning to his high school studies at Culver Military Academy in Indiana.

All of the Games family now live and work in Florida. If you thought that the author's flying adventures ended when he retired from military flying you guessed wrong. The author has said that if he writes an autobiography of his adventures after the Army and Air Force he will call it a semi-biography as things in his life have been so far out no one would believe the stories are real.

The author is over 80 years old now and remembers when he had a problem trying to convince the VA that poison ivy rash was caused by Agent Orange. Between fits of laughter, the VA doctors treated the rash, and told him that soldiers who were 72 years old should retire in Florida — not parachute into a swamp because of engine failure.

SHANGRI-LA VIETNAM

by Ben R. Games, PhD

A long time ago in a land far, far away, young men flitted around trees and villages. They flew over rice paddies and amongst rubber plantations. In the jungle they were like humming birds feeding on flowers. Shangri-la you are here.

The sun was bright and the air warm. Flowers brightened the dark green grass, and the land was peaceful. Hats of woven grass protected the men and women working in rice paddies while the young men watched from the sky. In the villages men in white silk shirts and dark trousers walked with women wearing white silk pajama pants under split silk dresses with the bright colors of a rainbow. The picture brought thoughts of love and home to the young men flying their screaming birds. Shangri-la you are here.

Young men of yesterday flitted around the towns and fields with the sound of the blades going "Wop, Wop." Voices in their ears from LZs were calling, "Come to me! Come to me!" It was like flowers calling to bees, "Pick me! Pick me!" Shangri-la you are here.

Fly like a bird close to mother earth, peek around a building, look over a wall, stop and back up or turn around. Never having to pay for fuel. Shangri-la you are here.

Suddenly a dark wall appears creeping steadily across the land. The fields are empty. The noise of children and bright clothing are gone from the towns. A flash of light, the darkness, the sound of thunder or is it the guns. It's all the same as the young men fly to the battle as moths go to a flame. Many are consumed. Wherever the young men touch the wall of hate and fear, hope springs forth. Shangri-la where have you gone?

FUUJIN

by Ben R. Games, PhD

The Great One created the Heaven and Earth. Then he built a Garden of Eden for his likenesses. One day he rested. The next day he looked down upon his garden and saw that the trees, flowers, and meadows needed  water for they were turning brown; so he created soft billowy clouds to rain upon them. When he looked down again he saw that the clouds had never moved or the rain stopped. The ground had too much water and was turning into mud. God called the Archangel Michael, and told him to think of some way to help His garden grow.

The Archangel formed a committee of Angels and told them that the Lord had said to help the garden grow. They decided that someone would have to move the clouds to where the rain was needed, help pollinate the flowers, and help spread the seeds of all the plants. When the Lord heard of the plan he called out, "FUUJIN".

On warm days I gently rock the baby's cradle, dry the sweat from a man's brow, and move the clouds where they are needed to water the crops. I help move ships, and make high waves for the surfers. I help powered parachutes and trikes fly. I even help sail boats to win races. I make dust devils in dry fields and play with leaves in the fall. I am "FUUJIN"'

Upon God's order I parted the waters of the Red Sea. I can change the shape of Mountains, and create floods. I am on duty all the time. I seldom rest and I can change the winner of sail boat races just for fun. I can destroy crops, towns, or just one building. I can make a fisherman laugh or cry. I am "FUUJIN".

Some call me Typhoon, Hurricane, Tornado, Chinook, Thor, but no matter what I am called everyone knows me, loves me, hates me, and fears me. I am in charge of making the clouds move, and in helping God's children take care of the earth. I am the Okinawa God of Wind, I am, "FUUJIN".

RICHES

The more you give
the more you get.
The more you laugh,
the less you fret.
The more you do unselfishly,
the more you live abundantly.
The more of everything you share,
the more you always
have to spare.
The more you love,
the more you'll find.
That life is good,
and friends are kind.
For only what we give away,
enriches us from day to day.

by Helen M. Games, MBA

****

Helen M. Amsden, the girl from Goshen, Indiana met and married Ben R. Games, the man from Elkhart, Indiana on the 5th of June 1943 in Fort Stockton, Texas. Just to be sure that the man from Elkhart knew what he was doing, she became a single engine and multi-engine pilot. Then when he became a test pilot, who landed with out an engine sometimes, she earned a glider pilot rating. Helen was awarded a silver medal for being the 86th woman in the world to fly a helicopter. She has flown as his copilot in Army BT-13, C-45, and B-25. Once in Okinawa, she flew as an RO in his F-82G fighter. In Vietnam, she traveled in his Chinook helicopter "City of Elkhart."

POEMS BY JEFF

TO BELIEVE

I write and I talk,
In rhyme and rhyme,
Everyday time after time,
Family and friends,
Wonder is it God sent?
Or is it just an accident again?
Poetry is a gift you receive,
It makes others wonder and believe.

WHAT I DO

Well-nigh or will I?
Could I or should I?
Why do I think why?
Will I have to try?
I continue to look up at the sky,
And of course I can never deny,
What I will share with you,
Reality of course as I do what I do.

Ben R. Games, PhD

WRITE IT DOWN

Write it down, write it down,
Your brain is like a computer hound,
It remembers the voices and hears the sound,
So write it down, write it down.
I don't know why I started so late,
But I'm glad I started, I thinks it's great,
So write it down, write it down.
Words are something that can be found,
If you think of something good, and you hear a sound,
Treat yourself good, and write it down.

****

JEFFREY GRANT AMSDEN is the nephew of Ben R. Games, PhD and resides in Goshen, Indiana. He is a member of the International Society of Poets, National Authors Registry, and the International Society of Authors and Artists. He has been published in 16 anthologies including, Sparrowgrass, National Library of Poets, Amherst, Musings, Iliad, *and* Voices of Many Lands. *In 1995 he won 3 Editor's Choice Awards from the National Library of Poetry.*

EAST & WEST BERLIN

Ben R. Games, PhD

1961

I was an aviation student in class 43-K at Fort Stockton, Texas where Helen and I were married. After high school, she ran away from her home in Goshen, Indiana so we could be married on 5 June 1943. Now it was October 1961, and we had just landed a new tricycle D-18 at the Elkhart, Indiana airport when the base operator notified me on the Unicom radio that an important phone call was being held for me in base operations. I was in the USAF and was on DNIF (Duty Not Involving Flying) because I was still recovering from my last assignment.

Helen's physical was still good, so we would fly multi-engine aircraft together.

In 1960 I had graduated from the Nuclear Officers School at the Air University, and my new military assignment was as a Nuclear Safety and Disaster Control Officer. What I really did was wear civilian clothes and carry a briefcase full of money. Whenever a nuclear incident occurred, I'd fly a civilian plane or helicopter to the area and buy all the land that had any chance of having radiation activity for the government. I've built a lot of parking lots in my day.

When I answered the phone, I expected to be told that another nuclear incident had occurred. Instead, it was my control officer telling me that there would be a US Navy transport picking up members of the 122nd ANG Fighter Wing at the Fort Wayne Airport the day after tomorrow and there was a seat reserved for me. Helen, our two children, and Duchess, our beagle hound, would leave from New York in two weeks for La Havre, France, on the US United States.

The 122nd Fighter Wing was equipped to carry atomic bombs, so I wasn't surprised by being assigned to France. I also received a phone call from the French ambassador who told me that Helen and the children's visas for living in their country would be delivered to Helen at the port in New York and that Duchess, our Beagle hound, was cleared to travel with them.

The Navy transport was a C54, and it made a stop for crew change in Charleston, South Carolina. While traveling, I was wearing a USAF Major's uniform and carrying a brief case filled with $20,000 and a flight bag filled with my clothing. My civilian clothing would be purchased wherever I ended up.

On this assignment, I knew that President Kennedy had ordered that no American military dependents would receive travel orders for Europe. I also knew that Helen and my family had been issued visas. I figured I must be headed for France just in case something went terribly wrong, but I hadn't been briefed yet.

Everyone had to disembark during the Navy transport plane's fuel stop in Charleston. The passengers were notified that no one could leave the operations area, and that the flight to Europe would be delayed for six hours due to engine trouble.

You must understand I worry a lot when routines are changed. It seemed to me that it wasn't engine trouble causing the delay. I thought it might be happening to allow the plane to rendezvous with someone. In times like this I attempt to change things in the hope that it will give me an advantage in case I have to become involved.

There were three USAF officers aboard and the rest of the passengers were AF enlisted men. Six of them were Master Sergeants (E-7). I spoke to the NCOs, and they agreed to be responsible for the airmen and to take orders from me. Then I told the officers that the airmen were under my command and asked if they would assist me. I put one in charge of feeding everyone when we landed, another in charge of locating quarters for them, and the Captain was asked to act as my executive officer.

The pilot of the transport notified us over the cabin speaker that we would be landing in the Azores at 2200 hours. Then one of the Navy sailors came back to give me a written message, and told us that we would only be on the ground for 30 minutes to refuel. The note was a radio message directing me to meet a B-47 that had just landed.

We had all deplaned to stretch our legs when an AP jeep drove up. One of the airmen said that General LeMay was on the B-47 and wanted to see me.

I took a minute to tell the Navy Pilot that we would be ready to continue our flight at 0800 hours the next day. He said the plane couldn't wait, so I instructed him to notify his command to have another plane ready for us at 0800 hours. After that I climbed into the jeep and was whisked away to attend a briefing on why I was going to Europe.

This type of briefing was not strange to me. The first time I attended one was during WW II, and it was by General Hap Arnold. This time it was during the Berlin Crisis and headed by General LeMay.

When the jeep pulled up, LeMay was standing under the wing of the B-47 talking to Colonel Bucher. He was mad, and had just ordered the Colonel to fly the number two position on the wing of the fighter wing operation's officer. He walked forward to meet me still smoking his cigar. He was chewing on the tip of the cigar, and it glowed in the dark. I remember that it looked like a light waving in front of his face.

General LeMay briefed me on what he wanted, and the only points that I recorded in my Journal were about the funds I would need in my job. He informed me that when more money was needed I should notify General Spicer. Also that I was to keep the French happy.

He gave me specific instructions about what he wanted done concerning a fighter wing in England that would be moving to Chambley, France. Then he informed me that Brigadier General Sefton would meet me when we landed and would see that I had all the support I needed from the Indiana Air National Guard.

We had moved away from the B-47 while it was being refueled, and it looked like they were starting the preflight check for takeoff. General LeMay asked me what time I had scheduled for takeoff of the transport and when the plane would arrive in Chambely, France. Then he asked how I planed to meet President Kennedy's order about dependants. I informed him that I had requested a French Prostitute ID for my wife, and it had been issued. I also told him that the French didn't consider a prostitute to be a member of a man's family. He just laughed.

***

The next year was full of adventures and sometimes misadventures. The French had drafted a young lawyer and assigned him as my French Army driver. Then they assigned a French Army Major who lived in Paris as my counterpart.

Our job was to run the base without the officials knowing it. For instance, once a month I would be arrested and fined for violation of French tax laws. I would pay the fines, and the USAF finance center would continue working under American laws.

Colonel Bucher visited my office one time and everyone came to attention except for an AP who was sitting on a footlocker next to my desk. The Colonel ordered the man to stand at attention, and the man told him that he couldn't unless Major Games gave him permission. I gave the guard permission and he stood up. Then Colonel Busher ordered me to open the footlocker.

It was full of American Dollars (about $200,000) that had been sent to me by General Spicer to pay fines and to pay the French Army for their contingent who helped run Chambley Air Base. Colonel Bucher must have thought that I stole the money because he had the US Finance Department bring in auditors from the United States. They worked for six months undercover trying to find out where the money came from and what was done with it.

About a year later in the United States the Army's Chief Auditor looked me up and told me that they had closed the investigation with a comment that I worked for an unknown organization that was helping the French Government. He also told me that they had just finished an audit of a bank in Chicago where they saw my name listed and had discovered that I worked for the US Government.

He said that they had called Colonel Bucher, who was now a Brigadier General, and tried to tell him that he had made a mistake. Brigadier

General Bucher wouldn't listen and told them that I had just fooled everyone.

B/G Bucher then told about the time when the Brigadier General from the Fighter Wing in England had visited me in France, and how I refused a direct order to allow the transfer of American dependents from England to France. What I had actually told him was that if Colonel Bucher would order me to move the dependents I would send them home. The Brigadier General from England knew that Colonel Bucher would never order me to do anything, and so did I.

The Brigadier General from England left the Colonel's office mad as a wet hen and told me that he would have General Spicer telex a written order that we both had better follow. The following day I receive a phone call from the Chief of Staff. It went like this, "General Spicer asked me to inform you that a telex was being prepared with his signature by the Brigadier General who's wing was moving to France. I am to tell you to continue following your verbal orders. Do you understand?" I understood that it was going to be another unsatisfactory OER.

To the day he died B/G Bucher never forgave me or understood that my third order was to protect him from making a big mistake.

***

One day I came to work and found a telex inviting Helen and me for a visit to Wiesbaden. When we arrived, I was offered a visa for us to visit Berlin. It was a gift that was impossible to refuse. I can't help myself; if it's too good or too easy there must be something I'm not being told.

We accepted the visas and checked out of the Wiesbaden BOQ, leaving our bags in the hotel. We had an Air Force car drop us off at the airport so we could be checked in. Instead of going to the USAF counter, I stopped at the Air France civilian airline counter and obtained two seats on an Air France flight leaving at 2200 hours.

Now we had time to go to the circus and still get to Berlin on the day we were scheduled to travel. We arrived in Berlin and instead of going to the American sector, we took a bus to the British Sector. After locating a hotel that had a room, we walked the streets of Berlin looking for a restaurant. We decided on Chinese food, and believe it or not, there was a Chinese restaurant four blocks from the hotel that was still open at 2300 hours. The lesson we learned was that German Chinese food doesn't taste like food.

At midnight in Berlin we were walking on a street looking at window displays. There were no cars or people anywhere. It seemed like a deserted city, then we heard someone call my name. It was a man I had worked with a few years before. He was excited to find someone he knew.

At first I thought someone had followed us, but after a few minutes I knew he was a little drunk and just happened to see us. He greeted me like a long-lost friend until he remembered his unpaid bar bill and darted back inside the tavern. I think he was peeing on the side of the building when he first saw us.

When we returned to the hotel, there was a new room clerk at the desk. When I asked for our room key he produced it while wishing us a good night, Mr. Smyth. I wondered why they hadn't asked for our passports when we first checked in. My guess was that a previous guest had checked out after two hours, and the room clerk had pocked the room rent. Helen pulled off the bed's bottom sheet, and we snuggled down under a feathered quilt.

The next morning we checked out and took a street car to the end of its line. We were still a long way from the Berlin Wall. There were a few cars on the street, and we hitched a ride with a German driving a new VW bug. He took us to within a half mile of the Wall.

A bus pulled up just ahead of us, and a group of well dressed men and a guide got out. A British jeep with an MP driver and two MP guards joined them and escorted the visitors to a tower that was close to a barbed wire fence about twenty feet from the Wall. Helen watched them, and then asked a British corporal if we could climb the tower that looked into East Berlin after the English tourists had left.

I explained that we were Americans who were visiting the British sector just to see how they treated visitors. The Corporal had radioed for a Sergeant and after they talked to Helen we were told it took six weeks to get clearance to climb the tower. Since no one was around, they agreed to wait until we were ready to leave and give us a ride back to the streetcar line.

The Sergeant loaned us his binoculars and after we climbed the tower we could see three large gray buildings and two guard posts along the east side of the Wall. There were no cars, trucks, or people on the streets. Nothing moved and everything just looked drab and dreary.

One of the towers was built as high as the one we were on, and it was directly across form us. I used to tell people that when I looked across the Berlin Wall into East Germany that all I saw was someone looking through binoculars into West Berlin.

When we climbed down from the tower I had the feeling that I had just seen a glimmer of hell. On the ride back to the world we thanked our British friends and I noticed that Helen was not smiling. Somehow, we both had come to realize that this was not a game.

We had to wait hours at the airport before our Air France flight to Wiesbaden was scheduled to takeoff. We wanted to arrive at about the same time as the USAF transport plane.

After landing, we walked over to the USAF counter and met our driver who had just arrived to pick us up. He never realized that we had used another airline. He took us to the Officer's BOQ were we collected our bags and put them in our old French Citron car with the French license plate before heading back to Chambley.

A year later I was contacted by an intelligence officer in the United States who said that he was trying to compete a routine report on our visit to Berlin. He said that somehow our names weren't entered on the manifest of the USAF transport plane. Also that the BOQ records weren't clear about when we checked in.

He said that they knew from the staff car driver that we had made our connections, and one of their agents had reported seeing us in Berlin, but his report only indicated that it was near midnight. I told him it was a mystery to me why everything seemed to be screwed up. Today I'm convinced that it really was only a gift from General Spicer to Helen and me for a job well done.

BEYOND the Milky Way

by Ben R. Games, PhD

Roswell is a city in New Mexico where many people believe a flying saucer crashed in 1947. There was a bank on main street there that found it could make more money as a bar, so it changed its name to The Bank Bar and had more customers than it did as a bank. There was also a civilian airport and a Roswell Army Airfield. Just outside of town there was a spring and low level area where water had formed a mud flat. The hot sun baked the mud until it looked like checkered blocks of chocolate from the air.

Benny Bob was now a young man and Aircraft Commander of a B-29. He still had his imagination, humor, and was always looking for a little excitement. One day he and his B-29 copilot landed a small Taylor Craft aircraft with side-by-side seating on the Roswell mud flat and the plane's wheels got stuck.

People from the city gathered to watch as the two pilots, one on each side, lifted the plane while running along side it until it started flying. As the plane started to take-off, the copilot fell face down in the mud while Ben threw himself into the cockpit so he was half in and half out of the little airplane.

He flew the plane with his legs and feet flying outside in the wind. The plane was headed directly towards the road where people were standing and watching. The little plane didn't have enough horse power to fly with its nose pointed up towards the sun.

As Ben was climbing into the pilot's seat, the plane nosed down, bounced its wheels on the road, and then back into the air it flew. There was no danger to the crowd because everyone saw the plane coming toward the road and they all jumped off into the mud.

Ben circled once before landing on the road to pick up his copilot. They didn't get into any trouble because the Roswell Army Airfield Base Commander thought all the phone calls about two of his pilots getting stuck in the mud were someone playing a joke. He didn't believe that B-29 pilots could fly like that.

The only atomic bomb carrying B-29's in the world were stationed on Roswell Army Airfield. The Enola Gay was parked next to the operation's building facing the hanger road. Benny Bob, who was now called Ben, was assigned as a first lieutenant aircraft commander for a B-29 in 1945.

***

In 1947 Ben was working as a pilot for Lieutenant/General Bill Craigie's Chief of USAF Research and Development. His B-25 was stationed on Bolling Field in Washington D.C. When the General was aboard the plane, he flew in the left seat as the aircraft commander. When he wasn't aboard, Helen, Ben's wife, or the crew chief flew as his copilot.

It was during this time that General Le May asked his friend Bill to investigate the report of a flying saucer crash at Roswell. General Craigie, Ben, and the Crew Chief left Washington, D.C., and flew directly to Roswell Army Airfield. After General Craigie toured the cash, they returned to Washington D.C, where he reported directly to President Truman.

While the General talked to the people responsible for the crash investigation, Ben visited with friends and crew members of the 509th Bomb Group in the Roswell Officers Club.

It was just like the time after the atomic bomb was dropped. If everyone who claimed to have been on the Enola Gay when the bomb was dropped had really been on it, there would have been over 200 crew members. This was no different, since everyone claimed to have seen the flying saucer wreckage or said they had flown over it.

All of the pilots at the bar were telling each other about the strange spacecraft. Their stories were so far fetched that even Benny Bob's imagination as a young man would've had a hard time dreaming up a better story.

Adventures of Benny Bob

Ben wrote in his journal about that day, saying that some day he would tell the story but call it "BEYOND." Its first title was to be "Beyond Belief", but 58 years later he's not so sure.

The red planet Mars is important for the survival of our civilization on Earth. Someday an asteroid from beyond our sun's solar system will again appear and be on a collision course with Earth. Today there is the means to tell when and where it will hit.

Earth needs a permanent base where spaceships can refuel and load nuclear explosives. To change the flight path of an asteroid it will be necessary to maintain a store of nuclear explosives on Mars for generations. For an asteroid track to be changed enough to miss Earth it may take a serious of explosive pushes over months while it is moving within the sun's gravitational pull.

The two polar ice caps on Mars are made up of ice crystals and dry ice that are needed to help develop fuel for spaceships. With a gravity of less than half that of Earth, a spaceship could refuel and load twice as much nuclear explosive for moving an asteroid as it could if it left from Earth.

There would also be no danger of nuclear fallout or radiation exposure for Earth cities in the case of an accident. The dust storms on the red planet's surface would cause problems with communications and visibility, though. This may cause the first permanent base to be established on one of the moons of Mars, Phobos or Deimos.

The cost to maintain a stockpile of nuclear explosives and a base on Mars or its moons will be tremendous. It may take the entire resources of Earth to save God's children and the world. To the question, "Can it be done, and will it be done?" The answer is, "Yes!" Answering the question of who will lead the way is harder. It may be Americans, Russians, Chinese or another group who will band together to conquer the new frontier space.

When the US Air Force investigated flying saucers under the Blue Book Program, Ben became interested in the possibility of a country other than the United States having the ability to save Earth when the time came. It was a strange thought, even for someone with the imagination of Benny Bob. Young Ben's plan was so far out in left field that he never spoke or wrote it down.

He prayed a lot, read a lot, and became an expert on keeping secrets. He became a business administer, electronics engineer, nuclear weapons officer, disaster control planning expert, aircraft maintenance man, bombardier, USAF, US Army, and MI National Guard Recruiter, besides becoming a Senior Pilot in the USAF and Senior Aviator in the US Army. He is often quoted as saying, "The best way to keep a secret is not to have one."

All the signs pointed to a new frontier and it wasn't going to be "go west young man." For humanity to survive it had to be Beyond the Milky Way. It was such a far reaching idea that while many writers, scientists, and thinkers considered other worlds, the concept was thought to be science fiction by most people. As a young man Benny Bob read, dreamed, and started thinking, "What If?"

In 1951 Ben co-authored a paper, while working with the medical testing labs at Wright Patterson AFB, Dayton, Ohio on how to simulate space—using pressure instead of a vacuum for training purposes. As a test pilot for the USAF F-86D program he has flown over Mach-1 many times and is a member of North American Aviation Company's "Mach Busters Club."

There is a constellation named Aquila and a star called Altair. The universe is expanding and galaxies are moving further apart. Space is not a vacuum but is made up of dark matter and dark energy. Man has walked on the moon and robots have visited other planets.

The Chinese, Russian military, and American scientists have studied individuals who have telepathic ability in the hopes of finding a means for communication over vast distances in real time. The ability to communicate in real time is necessary for travel beyond the speed of light if the people of Earth are to learn or gain anything from the experience or knowledge of the men and women traveling to other galaxies.

Experiments in deep sleep capsules, hibernation, and freezing to prolong life are being performed in many countries. Most countries allow the replacement of organs to prolong life today. Heart, lung, and kidney transplants are common. Eventually they may be used to prolong people's lives to over one hundred-fifty years, if the transplants are made at the half-life of the organ with an artificial replacements. Tomorrow is almost here.

Without women, men would have no purpose and most of all there would be no reason to seek new worlds or to explore the universe. If man is to travel beyond the speed of light, then women must help lead the way. Where men go, women will follow. Where women go, men will attempt to get there first just to prove that it can be done. If humans are to visit other planets and even other galaxies, then they must travel together.

Every now and then a soul is brought forth into this world called Earth who is blessed with foresight or is chosen to help find the way for God's children to greener pastures on other worlds.

What if there are other worlds with souls like ours living on them? What if they needed help? Would we not try to investigate and try to learn about them? What if they called our spacecraft flying tops? What if they had dogs to help them? God has given all his children the freedom of choice. We are truly responsible for protecting the Earth and all creatures living on it.

Ben R. Games, PhD

If a person looks through a telescope at a star or planet far away, they are looking back through time. Many politicians have tried to change history by rewriting it. They know that studying history is like looking through a window into the future. If they look hard enough they will find that this world is entering a new age which may be best understood as the age of Geo-feudalism. Instead of a king we have a chairman of the board, instead of knights we have generals, instead of vassals we have stockholders, and instead of serfs we have employees in worldwide corporations without national boundaries. No one can change the future by rewriting the past.

Traveling beyond the Milky Way will be humanity's greatest adventure.

AUTHORS PERSONAL INFORMATION

Ben R. Games, PhD, Major, CW-4, TCNA-6, flew bombers and night fighters during WWII. Then Jet Fighters for the USAF during the Korean War, and Chinook helicopters in Vietnam for the 1st Cavalry Division. He is a member of the North American Mach Busters Club and of the Distinguished Flying Cross Society and has 737 recorded combat hours. After 35 years he retired from military flying in 1978, and later became the manager of the Turks & Caicos National Airline.

He served in Vietnam as a pilot with the 228 Aviation Battalion, Company B, 1st Cavalry Division, and is a life member of Army Aviation Class 43K, 1st Cavalry Division Association,

MOAA, USAF Association, VHPA, DFC Society, National Guard Association of the US, Camp Grayling Officers Club, VFW, American Legion, and the DAV.

During his military service Ben was awarded the Distinguished Flying Cross for Heroism, Bronze Star, 14 Air Medals, an Army Commendation Medal with "V" Device, National Defense Service Medal w/3 Bronze Service Stars, MI Medals of Valor w/Oak leaf cluster, two Legion of Merit, Vietnam Campaign Medal w/1960 device, Republic of Vietnam Gallantry Cross w/Palm Unit Citation, and Republic of Vietnam Civil Actions Medal of Honor with First Class Unit Citation.

During the past fifty years stories of his adventures have been read by people around the world. They range from a child's Christmas story, biographical adventures, to science fiction.

Buy books at:

www.FideliPublishing.com

Angels

Angels drifting in the midnight sky,
Keeping vigil through the night
Twinkling stars and shining moon
Lend the Angels needed light.

Sun is rising in the east
Moon salutes, gives up his post
Dips into the ocean way out west,
Sun becomes the daily host.

Angels floating gently high above,
Silently like a beautiful dove
Watching children jump and play,
At closing of a perfect day.

Author
Helen M. Games

**Books by
Ben R. Games, PhD
may be ordered through:**

Fideli Publishing Inc
119 W. Morgan St.
Martinsville, IN 46151

Phone: (888) 343-3542
www.FideliPublishing.com

Ebooks may be purchased through Amazon.com, Smashwords. com, BarnesandNoble.com, Kobo.com, and through the Sony and Apple iPad stores.

MY GUARDIAN ANGEL is about flying during WW II & Korea. All pilots need a Guardian Angel and this was especially true in these stories. Autobiography.

WITHOUT PREJUDICE is an autobiography of an Army Aviator during the Vietnam War. He is married to a beautiful lady, and they live on a Fire Base called Bearcat. The story is about a Chinook Helicopter named the "City of Elkhart" that was destroyed in a fire fight at LZ Vivian.

POWERED PARACHUTE ZONE is a Coffee Table Picture Book about flying powered parachutes from farmers fields. It's all about being free.

SANTA'S SECRET is woven from the fabric of the author's imagination. The people are real, and they really helped Santa as told in the fable. The story is about how Santa Claus forgot the children of the Turks and Caicos Islands BWI. This is a Christmas Story for everyone.

BEYOND is a science fiction story about Roswell, New Mexico and the astronauts from Zoran. It tells how they came to earth looking for help in their war against the Altairons, and how an American pilot became one of their Battle Captains. This store is not for the weak at heart.

MONTANA'S VACATION is a true story of a black Labrador Retriever trained as a Guide Dog who is taking his Companion on a vacation cruise in the Caribbean. The story is being told by Montana, and it's all about his adventures on the Holland American Lines Cruise Ships, and how he helps his Companion find the poop deck.

SINKING OF THE CAROL "B" is a semi-autobiographic story told by "Montana" a black Labrador Retriever Guide Dog,. It's about fighting in the Turks & Caicos Islands Drug War, and forming a secret intelligent organization with a code that has never been broken.

DEATH OF A PATRIOT is a semi-autobiographic story told by *"Montana" a* black Labrador Retriever. It tells about how JAGS the Chief Minister of the Turks and Caicos Is was assonated in the secret drug *war* that saved his country from the drug cartels.

ADVENTURES OF BENNY BOB are autobiographic stories with pictures of the author's life in the wild, wild, West during the great depression and the building of Hoover Dam. There are also stories and poems written by members of the

Games Clan with a paragraph about the author's relationship to Ben and Helen. It's about how a young man developed into a warrior during the Great Depression.

CONFESSION OF A CIA INTERROGATOR is a nonfiction adventure story of a CIA Contract Agent in Vietnam. The Communist had a plan to trap the US Army in the Saigon area and destroy it when the Paris Peace Accord was signed. Bill Colby, CIA OIC, also had a plan to destroy all Communist VC along the route to Saigon and delay the North Vietnamese for two week to allow the US Army to escape the trap. Gilbert H. Moriggia, CIA Agent, was Colby's man in the field..

SOLO Class 90Z is the last Class Book of Army Primary Class Book of 43K at Fort Stockton, Texas during WWII.. It is a true story with Ray C. Murry, 43J editor, and the author Ben R. Games, 43J & 43K members of the GIBBS FIELD ALUMNI ASSOCIATION 20 October 1990.

JIHAD VIETNAM by Ben R. Games, PhD is a nonfiction book of the CIA 's secret war within a war to save the United States from the Dark Forces. The American forces used a body count of enemy soldiers to prove their success at winning a battle. The Dark Forces counted everyone, women, children, and civilians as well as military soldiers killed and they won. After the Americans signed the Paris Peace Accord giving South Vietnam to the Dark Forces, history records that the killing really started. 1.7 million Cambodians were executed, over 1 million Laos people were killed, and 25% of South Vietnamese were killed or had to leave their homeland.

GALAXY SLAVES is a Science Fiction novel and is a sequel to BEYOND. It is based on true facts known about the universe today, and tells how robots have developed into self thinking machines. It is also about how humans and robots learned to work together to save the human race. After the last great battle to prevent humans from being raised like cattle to be eaten, the robots went looking for God to ask if they could become a host for His souls.

BALLS OF FIRE is a semi-biographic and nonfiction account of a Chinook CH-47 helicopter assigned to "B" Company 228th Av Bn, 1st Cavalry Division, Vietnam. It tells how it got the name "City of Elkhart" and how it arrived in Vietnam. It also tells about the artillery raids into Cambodia and the Snatch and Grab kidnapping of Viet Cong for interrogation by CIA Contract Agents. The story is also about its crew and how it liked flying, Helen, the wife of its Aircraft Commander.

THE TERRORIST MIRROR is a nonfiction semi-biographic tale about a military mission in Vietnam where Helen and Gentle Ben took a convoy through a free fire zone from Bearcat to Phouc Vinh. It was the bait for a trap to entice a North Vietnamese Tank Battalion to come out of hiding. It soon became a race between the enemy, and 1st Cavalry Tanks. The bait was a platoon of Thai soldiers, one US Army tank, one armed personnel vehicle, a 2½ T. truck, and a OH-6 Loach helicopter.

THE BANGKOK DROP is a nonfiction semi-biography. It's about researching targets for B-52 bombers. The author traveled with a group of school children to visit a Cambodian Buddhist Temple. During the visit he would leave the Temple and seek out factories building antiaircraft guns. After returning to Bangkok, Thailand, the location of targets would be placed into a CIA Drop Box.

WASPs OF WWII is a nonfiction story of women pilots training at Avenger Field, Texas. It tells about a Army Flight Check Pilot who played a joke on one of the woman students who thought she was going to be washed out of the flying school and how she tried to kill him.

WHO STOLE THE TRAIN? This is a nonfiction semi-biographical story of an Army Officer and five soldiers racing the Russians to capture a Japanese experimental laser cannon located on a cliff overlooking the Sea of Japan during WW-II.. The race started in the Philippine Islands and went to Japan, then by Jeep to the rail line near Fujigaya Air Field where they stole a train for the run to Nikaho.

THE DIVINE WIND This is a nonfiction semi-biographical story of an Army Officer who worked in the shadows during WWII. It's also about how the Kamikaze Pilots were recruited to become human bombs and terrorists. Mostly it's about how the terrorists were stopped when President Truman learned that Shinto Shrines worshipped Hachiman the God of War.

BEN & HELEN 50th ANNIVERSARY Join family and friends as they celebrate the 50th Anniversary and Wedding Vow Renewal Ceremony at the MacDill USAF Officers Club. 5 June 1993. (Video)

DISTINGUISHED FLYING CROSS & SILVER MEDAL. This tells about the history of the DFC and is also a personal tribute to Helen M. Games who was awarded a Silver Medal for being the 86th woman in the world to fly a helicopter.

INTERVIEW OF BEN R. GAMES, PHD, MAJ, CW4. This interview was conducted by the staff of the US Navy Air

Station for the Pensacola Air Museum and the DFC Society on the 29 Oct. 2008. Dr. Games received the DFC for heroism and served as a Senior Fighter Pilot for the USAF plus the INANG. He also served as a Senior Helicopter Aviator for the US Army and MIANG. (Video time: 36 minutes.)

BEN & HELEN 67TH WEDDING ANNIVERSARY. Vow and Renewal at the VFW Post 9226, Ellenton, Florida. 5 June 2010. Pictures by Errol Fletcher. (Video)

www.ingramcontent.com/pod-product-compliance
Lightning Source LLC
LaVergne TN
LVHW011709060526
838200LV00051B/2821